Jackie Bailey

SELF Centered Leadership

Becoming Influential, Intentional & Exceptional

Jackie Bailey

Copyright © 2015 Jackie Bailey

ISBN-13: 978-1502441300
ISBN-10: 1502441306

It is with gratitude and love for my husband and children that I dedicate this work. You have each given me love, support, and crazy experiences to write about. The challenging times have brought me growth and made me a better person. Thank you all for being there throughout the process.

This book is dedicated to you, the reader, and your desire to be exceptional. Now get out there, and change the world!

Contents

Acknowledgments   5

Introduction: *Life is a Fishbowl*   7

Chapter 1: *What is Leadership?*   13

Chapter 2: *Sacrifice*   25

Chapter 3: *Empowerment*   47

Chapter 4: *Love*   83

Chapter 5: *Friendship*   109

Chapter 6: *My SELF Fulfillment*   127

The Rest of the Story   137

Sources   143

About the Author   149

Acknowledgements

It takes a fishbowl to write a book, and I'm thankful for the many fishes that helped my vision and mission stay afloat.

Special thanks to my daughter, Holly Aprecio, for designing the lovely cover of *SELF Centered Leadership*.

I'm thankful to my son, Cory Bailey, for allowing me to write about his experiences. I'm glad he's still here to read it.

Thanks to Patricia Klingler for helping my message to be more eloquently written and grammatically correcter. (Hehe)

It is because of the inspiration and support of many bowl-mates that I decided to write. Thanks so much to all of you!

Introduction

Life is a fishbowl

Three goldfish.

That was the prize my seven-year old and five-year old children had won in a carnival game. Thanks a lot, carny man! What am I going to do with goldfish?

I was not prepared for the endless amount of supplies I had to purchase for these free fish. I needed to provide the proper filtration, environment and food.

I couldn't just flush them down the toilet ....although I'd thought about it. Now they were pets. My children's pets. I was sure there would be a teaching opportunity in this circumstance somehow.

In the two years of fish ownership that followed, my children did learn something. They learned that MOM had to change the water in the fishbowl every few days. They learned that MOM would remind them when the fish needed to be fed. They learned that MOM would ensure the safety of their three pets.

Okay...I admit that I might not have taught my kids how to be responsible pet owners, but I learned a lot from those three little fish. In fact, many hours of my life have been spent writing about the lessons I learned from them.

Life, I discovered, is very much like a fishbowl. An endless search for the proper filtration, environment and food for yourself, family, employers, and friends. You get the picture.

Since November 2011, I've been writing a blog called *Navigating Your Fishbowl*, about leadership, communication, and the relationships we have with other "fish" who live or work in our bowl – the environment wherein we find ourselves.

I began my career as a dental assistant. A dental office is very much like a fishbowl. You're stuck in an artificially lit environment and occasionally glance out the side of your bowl (a window). You're typically with people not of your choosing. You constantly try to stay afloat in a quick paced, often stressful, atmosphere.

Over the years, as I've served in business and civic organizations and attended schools and churches, I've noticed that these places can often feel like a fishbowl, too. Heck, my own home has felt like a fishbowl from time to time.

The best way to survive the challenges of whatever fishbowl you feel stuck in is echoed in the wise words of *Dori*, a regal blue tang fish, in the Disney movie *Finding Nemo*.

Dori said, "Just keep swimming; just keep swimming". Very good advice, indeed.

In 2009, I started writing a book called *Navigating Your Fishbowl....Without Becoming Cat Bait*. The intended topic was teamwork and the dynamics of leading teams in a fishbowl environment.

I thought I knew about leading teams when I started writing my book. However, at the same time, I took on a leadership position in the nonprofit organization, Toastmasters International. In that five year commitment, I led and served 3500 members in a geographical District.

Over those five years, I led teams of various sizes. Some teams had as few as seven people, while other teams were as large as 100. It was a fabulous opportunity, and I gained exceptional personal growth.

However, I found little time to write much of my book. The very aspect of leadership I wanted to write about was keeping me from having the time to write.

Because of the vast amount of knowledge I gained in finance, budgeting, conference planning, marketing, creating organizations from the ground up, training and coaching, I found that the book I started to write five years earlier was no longer the book I wanted to write when I completed my leadership term.

I had a different message to share, and that would require writing a book on a different subject.

You're about to read THAT book. *SELF Centered Leadership: Becoming Influential, Intentional, and Exceptional* is about what I discovered while leading - that before you can navigate the waters of team leadership, you must first learn to lead yourself.

No one sets sail on an ocean voyage without first understanding how the sails and the rudder on the boat work. Anyone who sets out to lead a team, without first having the traits the team is expected to have, is in for a rough journey.

It would be like a parent lying in bed yelling

at their children to get up and get ready for school. A leader who isn't willing to do what he or she asks of the team, will likely not inspire the desired action.

SELF is an acronym for the traits of an exceptional leader. The sails on your boat are:

SARIFICE

EMPOWERMENT

LOVE

FRIENDSHIP

Get used to these words. They will be used frequently in this book. I invite you to read this book with SELF introspection, SELF awareness, and SELF centeredness.

I may have neglected to properly teach my children to care for their goldfish all those years ago, but I'm about to correct a mistake that most mothers make. I'm going teach you the exact opposite of a principle that mothers have taught through the ages.

It's okay to be SELF-ish! This book is going to teach you how.

Chapter 1

What Is Leadership?

Let's start by defining leadership.

The word leadership is ambiguous without the proper context. Leadership can mean different things at different times and under different circumstances. The word doesn't even distinguish between good or bad leaders.

Leadership means something different to each individual. I discovered this to be the case when I used social media to ask a simple question: "Define LEADERSHIP in one word"

Answers to my question came from all over the world and were different in many ways. Leadership meant something different to everyone. Here is a partial list of the answers, captured in a wordle:

Though different, all of the one-word definitions of leadership are correct. Each individual
would likely change their definition of leadership
based on their current experience and/or per-
spective.

I rest my case. The concept of leadership is
ambiguous.

Leadership is a combination of personal
traits needed at specific times to motivate
specific people to accomplish specific tasks. Is
that ambiguously specific enough?

It's tough to truly define leadership. It makes
sense then, to turn to a few well-known leaders
to learn their definition of leadership.

Following are some of my favorite quotes
about leadership. I challenge you to discover in
them *ONE WORD* that clearly defines leadership.

Here's a clue: you won't actually find the

word IN the quotes.

Don't read ahead! That's cheating.

As you read the following quotes, consider what *ONE WORD* defines leadership...

"A genuine leader is not a searcher for consensus but a molder of consensus" ~ Martin Luther King, Jr.

"If your actions inspire others to dream more, learn more, do more and become more, you are a leader" ~ John Quincy Adams

"A leader is one who knows the way, goes the way, and shows the way" ~ John C. Maxwell

"Leadership is the art of getting someone else to do something you want done because he wants to do it" ~ Dwight D. Eisenhower

"Good leadership consists of showing average people how to do the work of superior people" ~ John D. Rockefeller

"Leadership is diving for a loose ball, getting the crowd involved, getting other players involved. It's being able to take it as well as dish it out. That's the only way you're going to get respect

from the players" ~ Larry Bird

"Leadership is a potent combination of strategy and character. But if you must be without one, be without the strategy" ~ Norman Schwarzkopf

"The secret to success is good leadership, and good leadership is all about making the lives of your team members or workers better" ~ Tony Dungy

"Leadership is about being a servant first" ~ Allen West

These quotes are powerful and true. Did you pass the test? Did you find a word that is not used in the quotes but that clearly defines leadership?

I did. I found *ONE WORD* that can be extracted from all the opinions of others, and be refined into a *ONE WORD* definition. I found *ONE WORD* that encompasses leadership as a principle. *ONE WORD* that is unspoken, but clearly felt in each of the quotes above, and in every experience of leadership.

The *ONE WORD* is INFLUENCE

Influence is the power to affect change in the actions and behaviors of others.

Do you know any leader (good or bad) that didn't influence his or her followers? Leadership happens when we are placed in a position of leading. However, that is not the only time we lead. We lead by influence every day, in every way.

I recall a television commercial for an auto insurance company. The advertisement consisted of vignettes of average people witnessing others doing a good deed.

The influence of seeing others perform a good deed encouraged the witnesses to perform their own acts of service. I don't know how well this concept sold auto insurance, but it sold me on a true principle of leadership.

INFLUENCE

Our influence affects others constantly—for good or bad. We often have no idea when our example is influencing others.

The 10 most likely times you influence someone else:

1. When you are awake
2. When you are asleep
3. When you are alone
4. When you are with others
5. When you are talking
6. When you are listening
7. When you are showing love

8.   When you are exhibiting hate
9.   When you are living
10.   When you are no longer living

Since this list is quite lengthy, just remember three little words to sum up your most likely influential moments: ALL THE TIME

With the word *influence* in mind, re-read the answers to my social media request, and the quotes from known leaders, to discover how the word *influence* is the thread that weaves all the definitions together.

Remember the wordle?

All of the words in the wordle are synonyms for *influence*. Let's pull out a few of the quotes as well to discover the essence of *influence*....

"A genuine leader is not a searcher for consensus but a molder of consensus" ~ M. L. King, Jr.

How is consensus reached? Consensus is reached by two or more people *influencing* each other, and a leader who *influences* the result.

"If your actions inspire others to dream more, learn more, do more and become more, you are a leader" ~ John Quincy Adams

Inspire is just another word for *influence.*

"A leader is one who knows the way, goes the way, and shows the way" ~ John C. Maxwell

We *influence* others by our knowledge, experience, and example.

Go back and read the other quotes. I'm confident you'll see the power of *influence* in those messages. I challenge you to look for *influence* in what you see and hear throughout your day. You'll discover *influence* everywhere.

More than 90 years ago, Dr. Ralph Smedley founded the non-profit organization, Toastmasters International. His intention was to help people enhance their communication and leadership skills. That continues to be the mission of the organization today.

Dr. Smedley defined *leadership* as, "...the capacity to influence others to achieve worthwhile results".

There's that word. My favorite leadership-defining word. INFLUENCE.

How do people like you and me gain the capacity to *influence* others to achieve worthwhile results?

How can your *influence* become a force or power to affect change in others?

This book will answer those questions.

WE ARE ALL leaders. Each one of us influences another. This influence is either good or bad. Influence is the first quality we are born with, it is natural to our human state, and we develop stronger influence throughout our lives.

Consider how much influence you had on your parents before you were even born. It is very likely that when your parents learned of your impending arrival, they began to think, behave, and feel differently.

Since you arrived on the scene, you have continued to influence your parents and those who love you most. Influence is the first quality we are born with.

Oppression is the act of squashing the influence of someone else. We cannot be who we are meant to be if our ability to influence is suppressed.

Although we all have a natural ability to influence, this book will teach you how to take your leadership to the next level. That next level is *exceptional leadership*. Exceptional leadership trumps natural influence.

I define *exceptional leadership* as: Influence combined with intention to develop better and more abundant leaders.

It's important to understand the difference between leadership, and leadership that is exceptional.

Leadership uses natural *influence* to affect change in others. *Exceptional leadership* uses natural *influence* combined with actionable *intention* that inspires others to affect change in the life of someone else.

Exceptional leadership is not just about teaching someone to lead. It's about teaching someone to inspire someone else to lead. Exceptional leadership is the intention to develop more leaders, not to just *influence* followers.

Synonyms for EXCEPTIONAL include:
- Unique
- Remarkable
- Rare
- Uncommon
- Extraordinary
- Singular

How does a leader become exceptional? How does one use the influence of leadership to intentionally develop in someone else the ability to lead?

The answers are found within your SELF. Exceptional leadership is achieved when you master four attributes.

SACRIFICE
EMPOWERMENT
LOVE
FRIENDSHIP

Unlike influence, the characteristics of exceptional leadership are not automatic in their achievement. Sacrifice, Empowerment, Love and Friendship must be mastered in order to affect profound change in someone else. When your influence and intention become the catalyst in someone else's leadership growth, you are an exceptional leader.

An odyssey within your fishbowl is required to understand, practice and attain each quality of SELF.

I call it an odyssey because finding your SELF is much harder, and requires more work, than a simple journey.

Christopher Columbus did not discover America while on a pleasure cruise.

Note the difference between a journey and an odyssey from Dictionary.com:

Journey:...*progress from one stage to another.*

Odyssey:...*a long series of wanderings or adventures, especially when filled with notable experiences, hardships, etc.*

Exceptional leadership does not happen from one day to the next. Exceptional leadership is fraught with lessons, failure, experience, success, sadness, exhaustion, inconvenience, and even pain. Exceptional leaders are born from personal hardship with the intention to overcome.

By the end of this book, I hope you will be able to see your SELF in the composite of an exceptional leader.

If you are a parent, business owner, employee, student, manager, president, governor, pastor, or are in some other position of influence, you can, and should, become an exceptional leader.

Grab your oars; your compass; your life jacket; and your motion sickness meds. Be prepared for a wild ride!

Your odyssey to SELF has begun.

Jackie Bailey

Chapter 2

Sacrifice

Do you ever feel like a goldfish in a bowl, trying to navigate your way through life and stay afloat? Do you ever fear becoming cat bait?

A fishbowl environment can be both challenging and inspiring. When we want to be exceptional in that environment, our odyssey of SELF begins.

In the first chapter you learned that *leadership* is the use of natural *influence* to affect change in another person.

Exceptional leadership is the use of natural *influence,* combined with actionable *intention,* to inspire others to affect change in the life of someone else.

The #1 characteristic of an exceptional leader is Sacrifice. Your odyssey is about learning to master SELF, beginning with the mastery of Sacrifice.

To illustrate what Sacrifice means, I have included stories of three individuals who, by using their natural influence, accomplished exceptional feats. Perhaps you will recognize yourself, or someone you know who is exceptional, by reading the three stories below.

These stories do not suggest that you can only attain exceptional traits by doing what these individuals did. The following stories may help you see that by using your *influence* with *intention*, it is possible to become *exceptional*.

Nikolai Vavilov

Nikolai Vavilov was a Russian botanist and arguably one of the greatest scientists of the 20th Century. By 1941, he had created the largest seed bank in the world. His collection of 400,000 seeds, roots, fruits and genetic material held the future of Soviet agriculture.

Vavilov's seed bank was located in Leningrad, a city that Stalin had encircled the summer of 1941 in hope of starving the people out.

Stalin's plan worked. After two years of starvation, a million lives were lost. For those two years, Vavilov and his scientists had been surrounded by edible plants, but they refused to eat them.

Containers of rice, peas, corn and wheat were available to them, but all nine scientists and many workers chose death by starvation rather than eat the plants and destroy the preservation of these important genes for future generations.

Vavilov himself died of starvation as a prisoner of war in 1943. So tragic that a man with a mission to save humanity with food (and did), should die of starvation.

———

Today Vavilov's bank of genes hosts the largest collection of fruits and berries in the world. Imagine the knowledge, courage, and strength Vavilov possessed to achieve what he did. Imagine the Sacrifice.

Perhaps the Sacrifices of Nikolai Vavilov and the other Russian scientists will come to mind the next time you eat strawberry shortcake, or a piece of blueberry pie.

Vavilov's Sacrifice continues to influence our lives and behaviors. *Seed.The Untold Story,* a movie that highlights his mission, is scheduled for release in 2015.

Rick Rescorla

September 11, 2001 is a day that most Americans remember. Many heroes were born, and many heroes died, that day.

Sacrifices of the fallen were made on behalf of those

who lived. The influence of these heroes is still felt around the world.

Rick Rescorla was an American hero. His heroic act culminated on September 11, 2001 because of the Sacrifices he made prior to that date. His early Sacrifices allowed his final influential act to become heroic.

Rick Rescorla was a retired, decorated United States Army Colonel. It wasn't part of his job description, but he had been concerned about the security vulnerabilities of the garage at the World Trade Center in New York City even before the first attack on the building in 1993.

Rescorla was instructed by the Port Authority of New York and New Jersey to focus only on the 22 floors that housed Morgan Stanley in the south tower of the building.

In 1997, he became director of security at Morgan Stanley, where he maintained vigilant attention to the safety of the firm and the building. He held twice-yearly evacuation drills by the stairwell. The result of his service? On September 11, 2001, he was prepared to lead many employees to a safe evacuation.

Despite having received official instructions to stay put after the first tower was struck by a plane at 8:46 a.m., Rescorla told Morgan Stanley staffers to follow his plan. He sent them two by two, as they had practiced, down the many flights of stairs.

His decision and his preparation made all the difference. Although 13 employees, including Rescorla, perished that day, more than 2,500 employees of Morgan Stanley left the tower alive.

—

The word preparedness comes to mind when thinking of Rick Rescorla's Sacrifice. So does the word HERO.

Miki Endo

On March 11, 2011 a devastating tsunami hit east Japan. In the town of Minamisanriku, Miki Endo became a hero. Her words of instruction had a saving influence over thousands of residents.

Miki was a staff worker at the Minamisanriku town hall. As the tsunami approached, Miki could have saved her own life by running to higher ground. Instead, she used the community loud speaker to warn and instruct the residents on what to do, saving 10,000 people.

Miki's body was never recovered from the devastation. She was 24 years old, and had been married less than a year. Miki had much to live for, yet she chose to save thousands of people she didn't even know.

—

Nikolai Vavilov, Rick Rescorla, and Miki Endo had knowledge, courage and strength. They didn't set out to do anything particularly amazing. They did not know they would be heroes to nations, and an everlasting influence to generations. However it was their personal Sacrifice that clearly made them so.

I don't share these stories to suggest that leaders must be heroes. Nor do I wish to convey that if you do not commit a heroic act that you're not a leader. All of us are put into positions of leadership at one time or another, and rarely do we have an opportunity to be heroic.

I share these stories because Sacrifice is key to exceptional leadership. Inspiration and influence of others can come only through self-Sacrifice.

"True heroism is remarkably sober, very undramatic. It is not the courage to surpass others at whatever cost, but the courage to serve others at whatever the cost." ~ Arthur Ashe

Exceptional leaders and heroic leaders Sacrifice because they care about the success of those they lead, and they recognize the influence they have simply by being who they are.

What Sacrifices have you made for others? What Sacrifices by others have influenced you the most?

In his book, *Lectures on Faith*, Joseph Smith, Jr., founder of The Church of Jesus Christ of Latter-Day Saints (arguably one of the most influential religions in the modern world) tells us, *"....a religion that does not require the sacrifice of all things never has power sufficient to produce the faith necessary unto life...."*

Sacrifice of all things. That's pretty big. This doesn't just apply to religion, though. Religion, like a job or a position of leadership is something you are accountable to.

Have you ever considered your personal accountability? Personal accountability is more important than being accountable to someone else.

Sacrifice of all things means that, when faced with a choice of your own happiness, or the happiness, safety, or life of someone else, you will choose the latter.

More simply put: when faced with a choice between *your* WANT and the NEED of another, you will fill the NEED of your neighbor ahead of *your* WANT.

However, it is not wise to Sacrifice your NEED for the WANT of another. Sacrifice is giving up your WANTS for another's NEEDS. Stupidity is giving up your NEEDS for another's WANTS.

We are rarely asked to Sacrifice our lives in the way that Nikolai Vavilov, Rick Rescorla, and Miki Endo did. However, we Sacrifice our lives in the way we spend our time daily. Isn't life merely a matter of time?

If life is time, then when we waste time, we are Sacrificing greater opportunity, and we are wasting our life.

Relinquish a want to satisfy a need; you are exceptional and ready to lead! Exchange a need for something of want; you will soon have nothing to flaunt.

How do you know when Sacrifice is required?

There's an **APP** for that!
Actions
Possessions
Possibilities

The SACRIFICE or VICE chart seen on the following page provides a way for you to determine whether or not you're making the best choices when it comes to your actions, possessions, and the possibilities that lie before you. By answering the questions on the chart, you can decide what choice is best in any given situation.

In order to determine where you are currently, and where Sacrifice may be needed, honestly fill out this chart, considering that some actions/possessions/possibilities may begin as wants, but then become needs.

ACTIONS:
1. List all the tasks you perform in a day.
2. Who are you accountable to for each task?
3. What is the outcome of accomplishing each task?
4. Is your action based on a want or a need?

POSSESSIONS:
1. List the items you want to buy.
2. Why do you want to have each item?
3. Do you have money budgeted to buy each item?

4. Is buying each item based on a want or a need?

POSSIBILITIES:
1. List the accomplishments you want to achieve.
2. What does a successful outcome look like?
3. Who or what will support you during the process?
4. Is it best to begin now or later?

A blank chart is provided on the next page, and on my website EmeraldCityConsulting.com

Sacrifice or Vice?

Actions	Accountable to	Outcome	Need and/or want

Possessions	Reason	Where budgeted	Need and/or want

Possibilities	Outcome	Supported by	Now or Later

Jackie Bailey Emerald City Consulting www.emeraldcityconsulting.com

Sometimes it's hard to know the right choice to make. When you're looking for answers, it may help to ask yourself the question in four different ways. For instance, if the question is, "Should I buy a new car right now?":

Ask yourself the following four questions and weigh the possible outcome.

1. What is the potential BEST outcome if I DO buy a car now?

2. What is the potential WORST outcome if I DO buy a car now?

3. What is the potential BEST outcome if I DON'T buy a car now?

4. What is the potential WORST outcome if I DON'T buy a car now?

Some decisions are not always good or bad. Some decisions will have good, better or best outcomes. Those are the kinds of choices that require more dependence on Sacrifice. Always consider what you'll be Sacrificing to have/not have right now.

To have sufficient power to produce the life you desire, you may have to Sacrifice all/some things.

In my odyssey toward exceptional leadership, I mastered Sacrifice.

When I decided to break the silence of childhood abuse many years ago, I Sacrificed possible rejection, humiliation, friends, and even family relationships.

I've Sacrificed my own desires for the sake of an employer, an organization, even my church and family. Here's the thing....those Sacrifices have NOT weakened me. They have Empowered me. I have not lost who I am. I have found who I am.

Sacrifice enables you to grow and become who you are destined to be.

District Leadership

On July 1, 2010 I began serving as one of the top three leaders in Toastmasters International in Western Washington. I was the third-ranked officer of roughly 3500 members as the Lieutenant Governor Marketing for District 2.

One year later I moved up a seat, and served as the Lt. Governor Education and Training. By July 1, 2012 I was the head honcho, the big cheese, the lady in charge of District 2. I was the District Governor. Yikes! I thought I had been working hard the two previous years, but I was about to discover what busy really meant.

Because I never do anything less than 100%, I charged in full speed and set out to motivate and lead a team of about 75 volunteers in this very large organization.

That's only half the story, though. The earlier half began in 2009, when my husband had to close his architectural firm of 14 years. At its peak the firm consisted of four partners and 20 employees billing 2.2 million dollars a year. By the time it closed, two of the partners had jumped ship, and there were six employees left.

My husband Sacrificed months of his own salary so he could pay his employees. We Sacrificed our life savings to keep the business afloat. We ended up getting behind in our house payments, and we couldn't afford to make minor repairs.

In 2010, just one month after I began my four-year commitment to District 2 and Toastmasters International, my husband and I declared bankruptcy. We were losing our home to foreclosure.

From the beginning of my term as the Lt. Governor Marketing, I had had many sleepless nights of worry. It was a high pressure "job", but it was part of my odyssey to SELF and I wanted to fulfill my responsibility.

On a sleepless night in November of 2010 – just after our bankruptcy was final, I was working on the computer at 4:00 a.m. I heard noises in the driveway, and saw flashing lights through the stained glass window on the front door.

I ran to the door and looked outside. A tow truck was preparing to take my car away. I had never had anything repossessed before. My heart fell into my stomach.

"They're taking my car!" I yelled upstairs to my sleeping husband.

The tow truck driver allowed me to get my personal belongings out of the car before he took it. I was very grateful for his kindness – it certainly wasn't expected.

Back inside the house, I laid on the couch and cried. I wasn't sad about the repossession specifically. I was just sad about more loss. We'd already lost so much.

I had to quickly get over my sadness. I had a meeting that morning. A new Toastmaster club was forming, and it was my responsibility to see that it happened.

No one would have faulted me if I'd decided to stay home and mope, but I would have faulted myself. What positive outcome could there be from moping around at home while ignoring my responsibilities? None.

I borrowed my husband's truck and fulfilled my responsibilities, telling no one at the meeting what had happened that morning. I Sacrificed my feelings to ensure the job was done.

We only told a few friends about our financial plight. Our long-time friend, Gary, stepped up to help big time. He gave me a car he wasn't using. Seriously, he GAVE me a car just a few days after mine had been repossessed.

Blessings were, and are, countless. I can never repay Gary for his kindness. I'm confident that he'll be blessed for his Sacrifice.

A month later, on December 27, my husband's truck was also repossessed.

By the beginning of 2011, the bank had not yet forced us out of our home, even though we had not made a mortgage payment for more than a year. We knew what the inevitable outcome would be, but we had such bad credit at this point. We could not have rented a home if a potential landlord did a credit check. We had to stay in our home as long as possible.

My husband had not found a job in almost two years now, and I was trying to work at my business the best I could.

My husband's former business partner David owned a second home which he'd rented to the same tenant for several years. David's tenant needed to move in January. The home would be vacant. Also, David was doing some architectural work with which he needed help.

BLESSINGS. David let us move into his rental home. He knew our situation, and did not require a credit check. He also had work that my husband could do that would likely cover the rent, and provide a little income as well.

In February, during the busiest time for a Lt. Governor Marketing, we moved from the home we thought would be the home we'd live in for the rest of our lives into a house in a neighborhood we would have never chosen to live.

Our new home was half the size of the one we'd lived in for eight years. We tried to sell our antique furniture and other belongings. We ended up giving most items away. But we were thankful we were able to make a move ahead of the bank. It was nice to feel even just a little control.

During the months preceding our move, and for months after our move, there were days when I just wanted to stay curled up in bed, and let the time tick away. I was so overwhelmed with merely surviving that I was not sure in which direction to take a step.

I was without faith. I was without hope. I couldn't see a future, and that made planning more than a day in advance a constant challenge.

But I was keenly aware of my responsibilities. I knew

what Toastmasters' members, clients, and others were expecting of me. I could not let them down.

If it were not for my responsibilities, I would have just stayed curled up in bed. It was the service and the Sacrifice for others that kept me going through some of the hardest times of my life.

———

Sacrifice is powerful. Service to others is the cure for faithlessness and hopelessness. Sacrifice of all things has power sufficient enough to produce the faith necessary unto life.

I Sacrificed a lot for leadership so I could diligently keep my commitments. Nevertheless, I'm not complaining, because I'm very glad I took on the challenge to lead in the Toastmasters organization. I don't believe I would have had the opportunity to learn the leadership lessons I did any other way.

I had the chance to be the CEO of an organization of 3500 + "employees". Wow! Did I mention that every minute of it was voluntary? I was never paid a salary.

With all the Sacrifice necessary to lead District 2, I never Sacrificed my integrity, my religious beliefs, or my self-respect. Nor did I ever compromise on the goals I set out to accomplish.

I did not meet all the benchmarks I wanted to as District Governor, but I left District 2 better and stronger than when it was put in my charge. I'm happy with that. I'm so thankful for the blessings I received.

I was disciplined, dependable, and available. The Sacrifices I made gave me the capacity to influence others to achieve worthwhile results.

Is it any wonder why I believe that Sacrifice is an important trait to possess? Sacrifice is the very trait that allowed me to progress in my odyssey toward exceptional leadership.

I have always felt that the most successful, powerful, and likeable leaders are those who are selfless, but for the purposes of this book and your odyssey of leadership, I am suggesting that exceptional leaders are SELF-ish.

You can't be SELF less and be an influential leader. Sacrifice, Empowerment, Love, and Friendship are required.

Sacrifice is never easy. That's the point.

To become exceptional is worth the hardship; it's worth the challenges. No one can be exceptional without challenges and hard-ships.

Be grateful for the ability to Sacrifice. It's an indication that you have something to give! The act of Sacrifice will allow you to discover your worth. That alone is exceptional!

The following story is an example of a day that may seem typical for many of us. Some of the situations portrayed may not apply to you, but the emotions illustrated likely will.

Practical Application

You arise at 6:00 a.m. on Monday. You work from home in your consulting business. The week is fully scheduled, and you repeat in your mind the chores and errands that need to be completed.

You throw in a load of laundry, and then spend about 10 minutes on one chapter of the novel you're currently reading.

With your work-out clothes on you head out for a run. Thirty minutes later, you put the first load of laundry into the dryer, and start load number two.

In the kitchen you make a quick breakfast smoothie, feed the dog and watch just ten minutes of the morning news.

You hop in the shower. Thirty minutes later, you take the first load of laundry from the dyer, load the dryer with the second load, and fold the first load.

Finally, you start up the computer in your office to send out several emails to team members with questions, tasks to do, and instructions.

You notice several email replies. Questions and requests come at you.

Action needed urgently from Larry. Rather than send the emails you needed to send, you must first put out a fire. Your search begins for a document used several months ago, and now needed by Larry.

Your phone rings. Sharon needs help with one of her tasks TODAY. You are the only one to help. It will take a few hours to do. UGH! Okay.

Two hours later, you're back at your computer. You begin working on a marketing piece for your business. Oh, wait. "I need to find that document for Larry!"

Several minutes later – found. Reworked. Sent. Back to your stuff.

A text from Sam reads "Hey, need to talk. Get something to eat?"

Lunch already? Geez. Time spent with Sam is productive, but time consuming. Your ideas have provided clarity for him. He's ready to put them into action.

Back at your desk. your half-completed marketing project still sits on your desktop.

"Let me just get a few emails out" you think to yourself. Just then a Smartphone alarm rings. Yikes! Conference call in ten minutes. You quickly gather the necessary documents and materials needed to lead your team through a scheduled meeting.

Ninety minutes later, you are exhausted and mentally spent. But, you are scheduled to take dinner to your friend, Donna who just had a baby. You committed to doing this last week. UGH!

One hour later the lasagna is in the oven. It will be ready to deliver at the scheduled time on your way out to meet some friends for a late dinner.

While the lasagna bakes, you get back to your computer.

You send out a few of the emails so necessary to send that morning. You're on a roll!

Then a familiar sound comes from down the hall. Yep, by the time you make it to the source of the sound, it's too late. You spend about twenty minutes cleaning up dog vomit from the carpet.

As you complete vomit cleanup, you decide it's a good time to check the lasagna. WHAT??? Is the oven not working?

Its working fine. You just forgot to turn it on. SON OF A GUN!

You turn the oven on, and now realizing that dinner will be late getting to Donna, you send her a text letting her know. You also send a text to a few of the friends you were going to meet, letting them know you'll be there when you can.

A few more emails go out while the lasagna bakes – this time for real.

The subject line to an incoming email reads, "Urgent reply needed". You take a deep breath, and open the email. Roy, a coaching client needs your feedback on his presentation due in one hour.

You pick up the phone, and talk Roy down from his panicked state. He's going to do a great job tonight. Would be nice to be there. But…..Yikes! Lasagna!

Almost forty five minutes late you deliver lasagna, salad and rolls to Donna, the new mommy. But your hope of just dropping the food off doesn't work out so well. She is exhausted, the baby is fussing, her husband is not yet home, and the older child is hungry and in need of attention.

You spend time getting dinner on plates for Donna and her child. While they eat at the dining table, you try to soothe the baby with pats, rocking, and anything that will work.

An hour later, the dishes are done, Donna feels better, the baby is asleep, and the 4-year old is bathed and in pajamas. Then daddy comes home! All appear ready for a better night – at least when compared to the day they've had.

Looking at your watch, you are frustrated and a little sad that you missed going out with your friends. UGH!

You get home, and realize that the second load of laundry still needs to be folded. Once that's completed, you set your sights on checking off a few more boxes on your to-do list.

Then, your dog jumps up next to you for some cuddle time. How can you resist that? You can't.

———

Have you ever had a day that just didn't go as planned? A day when you felt nothing was accomplished? Does this feeling frustrate you?

The next time you have this feeling, consider the number of people you helped or influenced because of your simple Sacrifices.

Your self-worth is not measured by what you get done. Your worth is measured by the lives you affect.

Larry, Donna, Sam, and even a new baby

were *i*nfluenced by your Sacrifice. There is just nothing better than that.

Chapter 3

*E*mpowerment

In October 2013, *Forbes Magazine* published *"The World's Most Powerful People"*. The list of 72 were mostly government leaders, entrepreneurs, and wealthy CEO's.

This begs the question - what does it mean to be powerful?

Is power defined by strength or intelligence? Is it gained by controlling people, possessions and wealth? If so, this type of power seems problematic----it can be taken away by someone even more powerful.

If *Forbes* published a list of "The World's Most Empowered People", the list would include anyone who:

- Has studied hard and passed a test
- Has faced a fear head on
- Has overcome hardship

All of us who are striving to be exceptional leaders would be on that list!

It would seem, then, that the power to control and dominate others is far less achievable than the power we have to influence our individual and personal triumphs.

The ability for self-Empowerment can never be taken from you; it can only be diminished when your bad choices decrease your power to be what you want to be.

You can be Empowered no matter what challenges you face; and no matter what your circumstance.

Exceptional leaders do not dominate or control others. Their goal is not to create more followers, but to develop more leaders. They do so by helping others to discover the talents, skills and strengths they possess.

What is Empowerment, and how do we help ourselves and others to achieve it?

In this chapter, you will learn

- The three P's of Empowerment
- The five imitators of happiness
- Three ways to be empowered daily

Let's break down the word EMPOWERMENT. It has three parts: EM; POWER; and MENT.

EM is a prefix meaning "before", such as with:

Embryo: the origin of life
Embattle: to prepare weapons for battle
Embark: to board a boat before setting sail

You are the embryo of a *leader*, embattled for an odyssey and ready to embark!

POWER is defined by Dictionary.com as: *...the ability to act; the force to fuel and inspire.*

MENT is a suffix indicating the result or product of an action.

EMPOWERMENT is: *Action that enables or inspires a planned result.*

Does this sound familiar? It reminds me of the definition of exceptional leadership: *natural influence, combined with actionable intention, to inspire others to affect change.*

Exceptional leadership IS about Empowering others with actionable intention. It is the E in SELF Centered Leadership.

This chapter is dedicated to helping you discover ways to Empower your life, and the life of those you love and lead.

Action that enables or inspires a planned

result is accomplished when you apply the three P's of Empowerment

1. Preparedness
2. Principles
3. Promises

Throughout this chapter, I will be sharing stories that illustrate how the three P's will help you achieve Empowerment. The first story is very personal, and with permission from my son, Cory, I share it with you.

Cory and Bubba

The Ski Patrol had searched for Cory for hours after dark, in sub-freezing temperatures, at 5000 feet. When they finally found him, he was wet and inappropriately dressed for the conditions. His core temperature was 93 degrees.

A series of poor decisions had resulted in complete powerlessness for this 25-year old man.

Cory and his friend, Bubba are highly skilled skiers. Cory learned to ski when he was 6 years old, and has no fear of skiing.

After mastering several runs on the groomed hills that January day, they decided to seek for perfect, untouched powder that could only be found beyond the borders of the ski area.

Cory and Bubba had no map, no compass, no food, and no water. They did not tell anyone where they were going. Both of them had cell phones, but they'd turned them off to conserve power in their already low batteries.

About an hour into their spontaneous adventure, the un-groomed terrain became too heavily treed to navigate. Off came their skis, and a hike in waist-deep snow ensued.

Cory and Bubba traveled up and across the mountain to get out of the dense trees, certain they would soon merge into one of the groomed runs. After some time, they were both fighting fatigue. Then they made a fateful decision.

"I'll hike up to the top of this ridge to get a better view," Cory said. "I'll yell down when I get there."

Bubba rested, while Cory struggled in the deep snow to reach the top of the ridge. When he got there, he found another ridge. Hiking to that ridge only led to another one.

The sun was setting now, and Cory remembered his promise. He yelled into the dark forest below.

"Bubba!"

---

[1] Photo courtesy of Cory Bailey

"Bubba!"

No response.

I interrupt Cory's story to emphasize a few important points about Empowerment. Remember the three P's of Empowerment are:

1. Preparedness
2. Principles
3. Promises

They pertain to the situation that Cory and Bubba have gotten themselves into.

Preparedness

Cory and Bubba were simply not prepared to face the consequences of their decision that day. Without a map, they were lost. Without a compass, they had no direction. Without food and water they had subjected themselves to fatigue and dehydration. Without telling anyone their plan, it could be hours or days before a search is started.

Are Cory and Bubba Empowered or powerless? Empowerment is...*action that enables or inspires a planned result.* So, what do you think?

Principles

Principles, or core values are personal beliefs, guiding truths, and rules of self conduct.

Principles and values are foundations for laws by which individuals govern themselves in every civil society.

Principles are strengthened when followed; weakened when compromised. Cory and Bubba knew better than to break the rules. Besides obedience, these young men compromised on other values and principles. Safety, integrity, and wisdom to name a few.

Identifying and living by a set of values is Empowering. Compromising your principles reaps powerlessness. Are Cory and Bubba Empowered or powerless?

Promises

Promises and commitments are harbingers of happiness. Empowerment can only happen when we live true to the promises and commitments we make. Cory may have Sacrificed Bubba's safety by not keeping his promise to call back at the first ridge.

These young men may have undermined their ability to help themselves. And worse, they were less Empowered to help each other, simply because of an un-kept promise.

Turning their backs on the three P's of Empowerment, Cory and Bubba had not taken actions that would enable a better outcome.

Up to this point of Cory's odyssey, hiking had, at least, kept him warm. But Cory was now wet with perspiration and overheated. He decided to cool off by removing his coat.

I use the word "coat" loosely, as Cory was only wearing a thin shell, like a wind-breaker jacket, with a t-shirt underneath. Not the proper clothing for mid-winter temperatures at 5000 feet.

It was night now, and Cory had no flashlight. His perspiration would bring on hypothermia. His jacket was frozen, and covered in ice. Realizing the desperate situation he was in, he decided to call Bubba, which required removing his gloves, and exposing his hands to the freezing temperature.

The phone rang. Bubba answered. "Dude, where are you?" he asked.

Of course, Cory had no idea where he was. Bubba was with the Ski Patrol. He had made his way down the mountain to the ski area and had reported Cory lost.

Bubba handed his phone to a member of the Ski Patrol who instructed Cory to hang up and call 911. "They'll be able to triangulate where you are from your cell phone," the patroller said. "Leave it on, and stay where you are".

Obeying this instruction may have been the hardest part of Cory's ordeal. How could he stay still when he was now so very, very cold?

Not able to wear his frozen jacket and now, frozen gloves, he hunkered down in a ball, trying to keep warm. His exhaustion overcame him and Cory fell asleep.

That was a bad thing to do.

Have you ever "fallen asleep" during your odyssey?

Many times we can get so exhausted mentally and even emotionally, that we fall asleep – we are paralyzed and without direction. We become weighed down with the consequences of bad choices or bad circumstances, and we lose the ability to receive inspiration or instruction. (See *District 2 Leadership* story in Chapter 2 *Sacrifice*)

Even if we ARE ready to move forward, during these times of "sleep", we struggle to know in which direction we should go.

We can awaken our self-Empowerment when we refocus our actions on the three P's:

1. Preparedness
2. Principles
3. Promises

If Cory had more fully applied the three P's, he would have been saved a lot of grief.

I'm thankful to say that the Ski Patrol saved Cory's life. They found him, nearly dead at midnight. Those individuals who had the power to save Cory arrived in time. They brought blankets, warm clothing and food.

It is usually the powerless who are saved by those who practice preparedness, adhere to principles, and keep their promises.

Some of us learn from our mistakes, while others make the same mistakes until we learn from them.

At the end of his ordeal, Cory said to me, "Don't worry mom, I won't go out of bounds THERE again."

How comforting it is as a mother, to know that your son won't break a rule in just one particular place! UGH!

What do you think? Did Cory learn from his mistakes?

About 18 months after the skiing incident, Cory faced death a second time; this time, on a long board. Cory ended up with a bilateral skull fracture and a traumatic brain injury. The fractures on each side of his skull went through both ear canals.

Despite some hearing loss and constant ringing in his ears, Cory is alive and well. He was married in the summer of 2014. More importantly, he has learned some hard lessons.

It was again the Empowered who came to the rescue of the powerless. Just like blankets, warm clothing and food helped Cory overcome his ski injuries; prayers from friends, family and strangers Empowered Cory to overcome his longboard injuries.

Unlike many young people in similar accidents, Cory can walk, talk, and enjoy life. I'm very thankful for the power of prayer and a capable medical team.

Cory has always marched to a slightly different drummer, and is in fact, a drummer.

My husband, Arny, is also a musician. He sings and plays guitar, bass guitar and drums. He performs in several tribute bands, one of which spotlights the music of the legendary band, Styx.

Not too long ago Arny took a drum workshop from Todd Sucherman, the drummer for Styx. During the class, Todd told a story that further illustrates the Empowering act of preparedness.

With Todd's permission, I share his story:

"Early in my career as a drummer, I was contacted by another band that had a gig the following weekend for which they needed a drummer. I was available for the show as well as the rehearsal the Thursday before, so I accepted.

By Monday I received a tape of the 20 or so songs I needed to learn. I spent the next few days listening to the tunes over and over, even listening in the shower and playing along at every opportunity.

By the time Thursday arrived, I knew the material. I was ready.

I arrived early for rehearsal and had my gear set up well before the rest of the band arrived. When they did, I introduced myself and offered to help them load in their gear.

After all were set up, I asked if we would be doing the songs in the order per the tape I had received. They responded "Yes."

Arny Bailey and Todd Sucherman

I immediately counted off, "1-2-3-4" and drove right into the first song. I got the gig within the first few moments of rehearsal.

If you want to succeed in this business, show up prepared, show up early, and show up ready to help in any way you can."

———

Empowerment is about planning, taking action, and achieving the desired outcome. You are

---

[2] Photo courtesy of Arny Bailey

Empowered when you focus on the three P's.

Principles and values guide us in making decisions. If you have a belief in God, or at least consider the possibility of God, you typically learn values at churches, mosques and other places of worship.

I am Christian, and have learned the values of honesty, accountability, virtue, and faith. I've also learned that disobedience to these principles may bring undesired consequences. Truth is truth no matter where it's found. Even if it's in a grocery store.

Let Them Eat Cake

In 1981, I worked as a cashier at a small neighborhood grocery store. About 30 minutes before closing one night, a man came through my checkout line to purchase a cake on display in the bakery. The bakery staff had left hours before.

Many baked goods came down the conveyor belt at my register throughout the day, but I only saw them once they'd been packaged up in a pink cardboard box with the price written clearly on the outside. I was unfamiliar with the process the bakery staff used up to that point.

Thankfully, my younger brother, Brian, the pack-out boy on my shift that night, said he knew what to do. We took a field trip to the bakery to fill my customer's request!

The more expensive, delicate desserts were kept in a refrigerated glass case that was always locked when the bakery closed. My customer spied a square, two-layer cake that he wanted. It was a chocolate cake covered in white frosting, and garnished with red roses and little green leaves.

Having found the keys to the bakery case, Brian unlocked the glass door and slid it open.

I carefully took the cake from the shelf, put it in a pink box, and labeled the box with the price marked on the tag next to the cake. Back at my register, the man paid for his treasure, and appeared to happily skip out of the store.

Score one for customer service!

Fifteen minutes later, the man returned to my check-out line carrying the same pink box. He was no longer holding the box as if it contained the finest jewels in the world. Instead, he carried it like a football, and set the box down on my counter like it was about to be kicked between the make-shift goal post of the stores front doors.

"It's not real," he said.

Perplexed, I pulled back the pink lid, and saw that the cake I sold moments before had now been cut with a knife half-way through the first layer of the cake. The cake was still whole.

Realizing instantly what had happened, I looked up at the man's face. He was no longer smiling, and a movie began to play in my mind as I imagined what had happened in his kitchen.

I imagined how he had craved chocolate cake all day. Unable to shake his sweet tooth, he rushed to the store after work. He spared no expense to have what he wanted. He gets home, grabs a sharp knife, and...... Eerrrt. He tried again. EERRT. The cake is Styrofoam!

Do you know that some bakeries frost chunks of Styrofoam to illustrate the decoration options and prices of certain types of cakes? I know that NOW.

The bakery at this grocery store regularly displayed imitation versions of their most popular desserts. This may or may not be a common marketing method today, but it has taught me to be aware of possible imitations everywhere.

Think of all the ways we can be deceived by imitations - fakes that look so close to the genuine item we can barely perceive the hoax.

Counterfeits are all around us; and not just with tangible items like a cake. We can be deceived in our desires for the intangible as well.

Tom learned that happiness can indeed be counterfeit. When his marriage of two years ended in divorce, and his ex-wife obtained custody of their young son, he exclaimed, "All I want is a happy family that loves one another!"

Tom's desire was good and attainable. A happy family is genuine and worth having.

However, Tom and his wife had conceived their son while they were dating. There was no commitment to marry until the consequence made it a more immediate decision.

Tom became addicted to alcohol and drugs,

which he could not give up even with a baby to care for. His wife chose to be unfaithful to him, and Tom got even by being unfaithful to her. His unhappiness led to more alcohol and drug use, then more unfaithfulness.

He craved something delicious---a happy loving family. He tried to achieve his desire through imitative means. He purchased a Styrofoam cake.

Tom's actions, and those of his wife, were contrary to his desire for happiness. Tom was not able to Empower himself, nor was his family Empowered by his influence.

This is not to say that a person cannot change their actions or behavior, or that lives cannot be made better. Of course they can! However, consequences CANNOT be changed. Once a choice is made, and an action is taken, the consequences are set. We are free to make a choice, but we are not free to choose the consequence. Consequences can only be managed, but never undone.

Case in point:

Child Trends, a Washington research group that analyzes government data, published a research brief in November 2011 titled: *Childbearing Outside of Marriage: Estimates and Trends in the United States* by Elizabeth Wildsmith, Ph.D., Nicole R. Steward-Streng, M.A., and Jennifer Manlove, Ph.D.

The brief reports:

"Couples who have children outside of marriage are younger, less healthy, and less educated than are married couples who have children. Children born outside of marriage tend to grow up with limited financial resources; to have less stability in their lives because their parents are more likely to split up and form new unions; and to have cognitive and behavioral problems, such as aggression and depression"

These statistics show the likely consequences children suffer when adults choose to have families outside of a real marriage commitment.

In 2012, 40.7 percent of all births in the United States occurred outside of marriage, according to the Centers for Disease Control's National Vital Statistics report of December 2013.

Roughly 41% of families in the U.S. exist because an imitation version of family was chosen. Many of these children are powerless because their parents did not make Empowering choices.

Since family is the most important unit of any civil society, it is easy to see how counterfeit families can lead to uncivil societies. YIKES!

Every child deserves to be raised under the influence and love of two parents who teach by example the importance, strengths and unique qualities of each gender. Early family experiences shape the rest of our lives, and are the foundation for who we become.

Statistically, in the United States, family structure contributes to certain characteristics of a child's well-being. So says an article titled *Single Parent Households - How Does it Affect the Children?*

The answers are thus:

- 72% of teenagers who have committed murder are from single-parent households
- 60% of people who commit rape crimes are from single-parent households
- 70% of single-parent mothers live in poverty

According to the *Center for Law and Social Policy:*

".....On average, children who grow up in families with both their biological parents in a low-conflict marriage are better off in a number of ways than children who grow up in single-, step- or cohabiting-parent households".

The genuine key to happiness is a stable, happy, two-parent home. It would be imitation to choose anything less than this. I say choose because I know that some situations are beyond our control. Families are shaped by death, divorce, and many other factors.

On your odyssey to exceptional leadership, take time to get your house in order. Strengthen your family by taking action that will enable or inspire a planned result closer to the genuine article. My life has been empowered because of my decisions to do so.

By the time I graduated high school, my parents had divorced. Both remarried, adding 3 siblings to the family. Then my mother divorced again.

I suffered the trauma of physical, emotional and sexual abuse, low income and a lack of education.

However, I chose a different path for myself than the one I may have been destined for. I learned early on that I could Empower myself no matter the circumstances I faced.

I didn't choose my circumstances, but my choices Empowered my possibilities. It was through preparedness, principles and promises that I did not end up a statistic.

I put a stop to my abuse. I chose an occupation and put myself through school. I held on to my standards of honesty, virtue and faith. I was a virgin when I married a virgin, and have been married over 32 years. I chose the genuine article, and not the imitation.

The choices we make can undermine real happiness, while leading us to believe that we've found the genuine article. These "fakes" keep us from being our best.

Following are five imitators of real happiness. Many times they are decorated beautifully, just like that Styrofoam cake.

1. Tobacco
2. Alcohol
3. Illicit Drugs
4. Damaging Relationships
5. Sexual Promiscuity

Consider if any of these imitations are affecting your ability to be *exceptional*. If you are addicted, enslaved, or controlled by any substance, you have chosen an imitator of happiness

My advice: stop your damaging behavior now. Recognize that alcohol does not make you funnier or smarter. Tobacco, alcohol and drugs lie to you, while they change you physiologically. When you abuse them they make you less than you are.

Don't imagine that you can take more than a few steps into a cow pasture without getting manure on your shoes. You can't. Nor can you expect to experiment with even the most seemingly innocent substances and not have crap to deal with.

I invite you to read the story of Elizabeth Sleasman on ObitsforLife.com. She gave up her

self-power to drugs at an early age. Rather th
lead an Empowered life, drugs over-powered he
She died at the age of 27. (See #1 on *The Rest of the Story* page at the end of this book)

If you struggle with relationships, or if the same issues, arguments, and problems keep coming up in your life, you may have purchased a Styrofoam cake.

Most of us, sometime in life, have friends and/or family members who do not Empower us; or who do not support our desire to make good choices.

If you have inadvertently surrounded yourself with people who do not uplift you, or help you feel good about becoming an exceptional leader, then LET THEM GO.

Choose to be around people who want to see you live without imitation and with self-Empowerment.

There is nothing more Empowering than guarding your virtue. We come into this world with the precious ability to replenish the human race within a family. So many people don't honor that ability, and instead, accept the imitation version of a committed relationship – they give away the most precious part of themselves to someone who is not committed to their lifelong happiness.

I've already presented evidence of the consequences of having children out of wedlock or in one-parent homes. Run from the Styrofoam cake!

Abuse of tobacco, alcohol, and drugs; choosing to be in damaging relationships; and behaving in ways that may have unexpected outcomes, are five ways that happiness can be imitated. These are not the only ways we can undermine our self-Empowerment.

The way you manage your time, and even your entertainment choices may be keeping you from achieving self-Empowerment. You may be participating in activities that are imitation.

ProCon.org, an independent, nonpartisan, non-profit organization that provides the pros and cons of 51 controversial issues, reports that in 2009:

- 68% of American households played computer/video games
- 49% of game players were between 18-49 years old
- 26% were 50 and older
- 25% were 18 and younger

First of all, is there nothing better to do than play video games?

Secondly, how does playing video games rank when measured with the three P's of Empowerment?

In 2008 the top three computer/video games were:
- *Guitar Hero*
- *Halo3*
- *Madden NFL*

Can you spot the imitations?

Guitar Hero is an obvious imitation. Go take actual guitar lessons, people! Improving your musical talents and skills is valuable, and very Empowering - much more Empowering than participating in the counterfeit version.

Halo3 is just a shoot-'em up, war and defense kind of game that, in my opinion downplays the horror of war and death. It desensitizes us to violence, and gives us a counterfeit sense of power. It is an imitation version of joining the military of your country and fighting for causes such as freedom, safety and liberty.

If you want to be skilled at marksmanship, take classes at a shooting range and become a responsible gun owner. Providing safety and security for yourself and family is Empowering. That is the genuine article. Sitting in your living room staring at a screen and firing at human-shaped targets is imitation.

The third game on the list according to ProCon.org is *Madden NFL*. Imitation? Good grief---go outside and play football with your friends! Your friendships and physical health will be strengthened. Why play a make-believe game when you can play a game for real, with very little skill or cost?

The problem with these Mature-Audience rated games is that the games may just imitate power to kids. There is evidence of this.

Pro Con.org compared the rates of problem behaviors in youth who played Mature-rated games and those who did not. Some of the results are as follows:

- Of boys who had hit or beat someone up, 60% of them played M-rated games, while 39% had not
- Of girls who damaged property just for fun, 15% played M-rated games, 5% had not
- Of boys who got into trouble with a teacher at school, 60% played M-rated games, 39% had not

Clearly, counterfeit scenarios and imitation behaviors do have an effect on our Empowerment abilities. I suggest the following genuine activities instead of video/computer games. These actions are Empowering:

1. Learn a new skill. Take a class in art, cooking, automotive repair, music, etc.

2. Increase your knowledge. Go to school; get certified in something that will further your career and make you more valuable to your employer.

3. Serve as a volunteer. Choose a cause you're passionate about and Sacrifice a few hours of your time to Empower others.

Personal growth will bring opportunities you can't even imagine, and will allow you to identify true happiness when you see it.

"The way you think, the way you behave, the way you eat, can influence your life by 30 to 50 years." ~ Deepak Chopra

I was drawn to that quote because he used *influence*. You know by now how much I like that word, and I also like to eat. So let's talk about food for a moment.

One of the easiest ways to Empower yourself is through fueling your body with healthy foods and healthy activities. Provided, of course, that you're eating REAL food.

I'm going to wax scientific for a moment because this is important for you to know. Genetically modified plants have had bacteria and viruses forced into their DNA.

This genetic engineering transfers genes across natural species barriers by shooting genes into cells or by using bacteria to invade the cell with DNA that has never been in the human food supply.

The altered cell is then cloned into a plant. We're eating these plants, and we're eating foods that contain these plants. We may not be eating Styrofoam, but possibly something even worse.

According to the *Institute of Responsible Technology*, as of May 2010, the following crops, foods and ingredients have been genetically modified using the method(s) I just described:

- Soy (94%)
- Cotton (90%)
- Canola (90%)
- Sugar beets (95%)
- Corn (88%)
- Hawaiian Papaya (50%+)

Other sources of genetically modified organics include:
- Dairy products from cows injected with the GM hormone rbGH
- Meat, eggs, and dairy products from animals that have eaten GM feed
- Food additives, enzymes, flavorings, and processing agents, including aspartame and rennet used to make hard cheeses
- Honey and bee pollen that may have GM sources of pollen

Consider the many ingredients derived from soy and corn, which are almost entirely genetically modified:

- Soy flour
- Soy protein
- Tofu

- Corn flour
- Corn starch
- Cornmeal

Yikes! Check the ingredients of your favorite foods. My guess is that you're eating more genetically modified foods than you might realize. Styrofoam never tasted so good!

In 2009, the American Academy of Environmental Medicine (AAEM) wrote:

"Several animal studies indicate serious health risks associated with genetically modified (GM) food; including infertility, immune problems, accelerated aging, faulty insulin regulation, and changes in major organs and the gastrointestinal system. The AAEM has asked physicians to advise all patients to avoid GM foods".

Not only are you likely eating imitation foods, but those foods are causing your body to function counter to its genetic makeup.

The foods you eat may actually be limiting your ability to have children, live disease free, and feel well daily. Eating genetically modified foods can be undermining your Empowerment.

Painfully Clear

For more than 28 years, I have suffered with a chronic, painful condition called Fibromyalgia. In all that time, no doctor ever suggested my diet might contributed to my pain.

However, I recently changed my diet. This change has decreased my pain, increased my energy, and improved my sleep. I also lost about 30 pounds. Talk about Empowerment!

Prior to this Empowering change, I had developed such intense and constant pain in my right shoulder that I was certain surgery was probable. I could not recall an incident when an injury occurred, but the pain was consistent with a rotator cuff injury.

J.J. Virgin, the author of *The Virgin Diet,* writes that many genetically modified foods we eat are likely culprits of America's weight gain, hormone imbalances, allergies, chronic pain, diabetes, and other common conditions seen in the American population. She suggests that there are seven foods most likely to cause problems for individuals who have developed intolerance to them, and that these foods could be exacerbating other conditions.

How do you prove a principle to be true? You test it. You live the principle and track the outcome.

Three days after I stopped eating the seven foods suggested by J.J. Virgin, my shoulder pain was completely gone, and I had no need for the daily pain medication I was taking for my Fibromyalgia. One month later, I had lost 10 pounds, was feeling energized and sleeping better.

Even after not eating those foods for six months, I continued to lose weight and noticed other health benefits. The truth of Ms. Virgin's message was proven, and I have been Empowered with better health!

———

The foods I have given up are gluten, corn,

dairy, eggs, soy, peanuts, tomatoes and sugar. Knowing the foods to give up is not enough to change your diet. You must learn how to find the right foods as well. I suggest you read *"The Virgin Diet"* for the important information it contains.

When better health provides opportunities for a more enjoyable life, Empowerment is the outcome.

I will provide just one more way for you to Empower yourself and others. It is through your communication.

Think about the ways our language has changed since the World Wide Web became part of our daily lives. We now speak Twitterese, write Textican, and practice Postology.

We all have important, valuable messages to share with each other. The language we use to communicate will either give our message more impact, or undermine its importance. Let me show you what I mean.

Dr. Martin Luther King, Jr gave a speech in 1963 that has become iconic in its message and inspiring in its content.

In one part of his speech, Dr. King said,

"I say to you today my friends, though, even though we face the difficulties of today and tomorrow, I still have a dream. It is a dream

deeply rooted in the American dream. I have a dream that one day this nation will rise up, live out the true meaning of its creed: 'We hold these truths to be self-evident, that all men are created equal'".

What if Dr. King had used language in his speech that has become accepted as slang today? What impact would that have had on his message?

Using today's social media English, Dr. King's speech may have sounded like this....

"Hey dudes, it's kinda like, well, like t'day and t'mara are gonna suck. Ya know, I was thinkin'. I was thinkin' 'bout, da 'merican dream 'n ever'thing. It'd be so sick if our country do what it said 'bout men bein' equal 'n ever'thing."

The intent of Dr. King's message would have been the same, but the uninspiring nature of his delivery would have diminished his credibility. His audience would not have been as moved, and the behavior change of a nation would not have taken place.

The language with which we choose to communicate with, matters.

Here's a different scenario. What if Dr. King spoke as he did in 1963, but instead of wearing a suit, was wearing sagging jeans, a t-shirt and baseball cap—worn sideways?

Would Dr. King have been taken seriously? Would his message have been as well received?

I admit these example are extreme and may even border on ridiculous. I don't share them to stereotype anyone, nor do I wish to make light of Dr. King's message.

I invite you to seriously ponder the following questions:

1. Have YOU ever been treated differently because you dressed a certain way?

2. Have YOU ever treated someone else differently because of the way they looked or dressed?

The way you present yourself matters when communicating your message. More importantly, you may be communicating the wrong message because of the way you speak, act or dress.

Where in The Mall is Your Mother?

When my daughter was 11 years old, she and a group of her friends wanted to play a game called, "Where in the Mall is Your Mother?" The objective of the game was for each daughter to identify her mother (who would be in disguise) in a crowded shopping mall.

Each of the mothers, myself included, went to the mall in our disguises, and arrived before the girls did. They arrived shortly after, and each began looking for her mother.

I applied a mascara-induced mustache on my face. I donned a pair of baggy jeans, big black shoes, and a hooded sweatshirt with the hood over a baseball cap. I also wore sunglasses.

The following picture is a recreation of how I looked at the mall that day.

I didn't want to walk too much, because I would surely give myself away. And since the rules stated that I could not go into any of the stores, I found a wall to lean against directly across from a beauty salon.

It wasn't long before the women in the beauty salon began to point in my direction, talk amongst themselves and then look back at me. I was clearly making them uncomfortable, so I moved a little further down the mall.

One of the girls in our group approached me. She sized

me up, came closer, and asked, "Pardon me, do you have the time?"

This was the key phrase, that if asked by our own daughter, we were to reveal ourselves.

This was not my daughter, and therefore I wasn't required to reveal my identity. I answered back in a very low, rough voice, "Time to leave me alone."

My daughter's friend squealed a little as she jumped back. Then she apologized and quickly walked away.

I was eventually found out, and my daughter and the rest of the mothers and daughters met in the designated location once the game was over. As we were laughing about our disguises and sharing stories, a shopper approached me.

She asked, "Who are you?"

Taking my sunglasses and hat off, and removing the cap to display my long hair, I confessed, "I'm just playing a game with my daughter."

The shopper said, "The police were called because of you, and there are officers in the mall right now watching you." She added, "You scared some ladies in a beauty salon."

I had no evil intent. I was just playing a game.

———

Discrimination? Unfair judgment? Incorrect assumptions? All of these conclusions can be drawn from this experience, and I've pondered at great length the most valuable lesson I can learn from it.

I believe it all boils down to this truth—my communication was confusing. My message did not match my behavior. Because it was so confusing, I actually caused fear in my "audience".

You are Empowered when you speak your message without jargon, fillers, and confusing or unnecessary words. You are Empowered when your actions match your message. You are Empowered when people see you as credible.

The importance of your message won't matter if no one is listening. The importance of your message won't matter if it's not understood. Define your message; deliver it purposefully; and dress for communication success.

You can be Empowered daily when you make better choices in the areas of:

- Entertainment and time management
- Health and diet
- Communication and credibility

This chapter has answered three questions.

1. What is self-Empowerment?
2. Why is self-Empowerment necessary?
3. How can I Empower myself?

Empowerment is.... *action that enables or inspires a planned result.*

Consider yourself the embryo of a leader, embattled for an odyssey and ready to embark!

We will all be given opportunity to lead in our homes, careers, school, and among our friends and peers. Understanding ourselves, our strengths and our weaknesses will be the oars we use on our odyssey. We can only Empower the ones we love if we Empower ourselves first.

You Empower your life when you avoid the five imitators of happiness, when you apply the three P's of Empowerment, and when you make better choices regarding entertainment and time management; diet and health; and communication.

You will be Empowered when you intentionally make the right choices. In turn, your action and influence will Empower those you Love.

We can be Empowered no matter what challenges we face; and no matter what our circumstance.

"You must become the change you want to see...You may never know what results come of your actions, but if you do nothing there will be no result". ~ Mahatma Gandhi

Jackie Bailey

Chapter 4

Love

There are as many ways to Love as there are people on planet Earth. What is Love to one person might feel like respect, admiration, or pity to another. There are no meters that measure Love, and no way to confirm that someone is feeling Love.

Although many poets, playwrights and musicians have written about Love, the emotion itself is very personal. You are the only one who knows how it feels when you experience Love.

If you are to become an *exceptional leader*, you must understand how it feels to Love, and why it is important to Love.

Unfortunately, the odyssey to SELF will likely be fraught with events and experiences that will test your Love. Leadership tests not only your Love of self, but Love for others.

I'm not speaking about romantic Love. The type of Love needed to lead and influence others is a charitable Love; a compassionate Love; a brotherly Love.

Love has been the topic of many philosophical discussions. As a Christian, I learned the philosophy of Love from the Bible and other scriptures. In *The New Testament,* Paul speaks about charity to the people of Corinth. Charity and the type of Love I will address in this chapter are interchangeable.

1st Corinthians 13:1-8

1. Though I speak with the tongues of men and of angels, and have not charity, I am become as sounding brass, or a tinkling cymbal.

2. And though I have the gift of prophecy, and understand all mysteries, and all knowledge; and though I have all faith, so that I could remove mountains, and have not charity, I am nothing.

3. And though I bestow all my goods to feed the poor, and though I give my body to be burned, and have not charity, it profiteth me nothing.

4. Charity suffereth long, and is kind; charity envieth not; charity vaunteth not itself, is not puffed up,

5. Doth not behave unseemly, seeketh not her own, is not easily provoked, thinketh no evil;

6. Rejoiceth not in iniquity, but rejoiceth in the truth;

7. Beareth all things, believeth all things, hopeth all things, endureth all things.

8. Charity never faileth;

<u>Charity never faileth.</u> We can possess many qualities; we can develop talents and skills; we can seek for the highest education possible; but if we are not charitable, and if we do not Love, nothing else matters.

If you're like me, you want to be successful in all you do. And, like me, you've probably also learned that success does not come without failure.

Thomas Edison was told by his teacher, "You're too stupid to learn anything."

Edison then went on to hold more than 1000 patents and invented life-changing devices like the phonograph, electric lamp, and movie camera.

Oprah Winfrey was fired from her first television anchor job. Forbes now estimates her worth to be 2.9 billion dollars, and she's the undisputed queen of television talk shows.

Walt Disney was told by a newspaper editor that he "...lacked imagination and had no good ideas".

However, my childhood, and those of millions of children in the last 50 years, have been enhanced by the talents and ideas of Mr. Disney.

These are examples of failure (or at least, perceived failure at the time) that is sometimes experienced before success comes to fruition.

We may fail, or be only partly successful at the goals we attempt to reach, or in the accomplishments we set out to achieve. Most of us will not invent a life-changing device, or become the king or queen of talk-show television.

But the truth is - we can be 100% successful in how we Love and in the charity we show to others. Feeling Love, and acting out of Love is NEVER a failure.

CHARITY NEVER FAILETH.

An exceptional leader will strive to make Love and charity his or her greatest talents.

"I sought to hear the voice of God and climbed the topmost steeple, but God declared: 'Go down again – I dwell among the people'." ~ John Henry Newman

"You will get all you want in life if you help enough other people get what they want." ~ Zig Ziglar

You can be 100% successful in charitable, compassionate, brotherly Love. The reason success comes in this way is because of how you influence those you Love.

The rest of this chapter will help you discover how to Love and be an influence for good through charity and brotherly Love.

"There are two basic motivating forces: fear and love. When we are afraid, we pull back from life. When we are in love, we open to all that life has to offer with passion, excitement, and acceptance.

We need to learn to love ourselves first, in all our glory and our imperfections. If we cannot love ourselves, we cannot fully open our ability to love others or our potential to create." ~ John Lennon

There you have it. Step one: LOVE YOUR-SELF.

I know, I know, I'm starting off with the hardest one. Loving yourself is perhaps the greatest task we have in life. It has been for me.

It seems to me that the people who have the hardest time Loving themselves are the same people who felt unloved as children. Childhood is certainly the making of us. The hard part is not allowing childhood to be the breaking of us.

Even though Loving ourselves is the first step, I found that it was my Love for someone else that kept me from being completely broken.

Love is all you need

I had been married for four years and had two children when my self-hatred began to break me. Many survivors of childhood sexual abuse cope by blocking their memories of the abuse. I had not coped with my abuse that way. I had not blocked any memories. I had never told anyone of my abuse, but I had never forgotten.

I never had a reason to tell anyone. At least not until my

abuser had his own child. That was what set me off. I could not remain silent now that a child was threatened by the same abuser. Keeping silent had served me well until then, but now my silence could allow harm to come to someone else. Love for a child forced me to face the hatred I had for myself.

Self-hatred coupled with an immediate, uncontrollable threat forced all my ugly feelings to gush out at once. I was angry. I was sad. I was frightened. I was ashamed. I was lonely. I did not believe I could face my family and my abuser with the ugly truth.

Suicide seemed to be the easiest solution. I wouldn't have to shame myself, or my family, or even my abuser. Everyone would be better off if I just crawled under a rock and never came back.

Everyone except the child of the abuser.

And what about MY children? Who would raise my children? Who would protect THEM from possible abuse?

Love for another person prevailed over self-hatred. I Loved my children more than I hated myself. I realized that I would need to go through the shame, and the pain, and the fear so that my children and my abusers child would be protected.

It was perhaps the hardest time in my life, and I wasn't even 25 years old. I didn't know I was on an odyssey to SELF then, but I certainly was.

I Sacrificed emotional energy to open up deep, infected scars so I could begin to heal from the abuse. I knew that if I could accomplish my ultimate goal – to confront my abuser face to face – I would be Empowered beyond where I could then see.

LOVE was the only reason I even made the attempt. LOVE would be the saving grace for myself and many others.

During group therapy and support, I became friends with other survivors, and even deepened the friendship I had with my husband.

—

It was indeed my SELF-ish behavior that led me through the hardest ordeal of my life. Little did I know it would only be the beginning of my odyssey.

I have learned what the Apostle Paul taught: "Love bears all things, believes all things, hopes all things, and endures all things."

How does one achieve self-Love? I view it as a process of four steps, using the acronym SAFE.

Service-Acceptance-Forgiveness-Engagement

Let's take a look at each of these steps. They will help you not only Love yourself, but Love others as well.

Service ~

"The best way to find yourself is to lose yourself in the service of others." ~ Mahatma Gandhi

There has never been a challenge I've faced in all my 50 years that did not seem lighter when I forgot myself and served someone else. And there has never been a circumstance when my challenges got worse because I spent too much time doing something for someone else.

Service to others develops a sense of self-worth. We grow to Love ourselves when we Love and serve someone who needs us. When we perform even one small deed, our Love for the recipient grows. We feel greater hope and peace – we feel that we have value. That is the seed of self-Love.

"Everybody can be great....because anybody can serve. You don't have to have a college degree to serve. You don't have to make your subject and verb agree to serve. You only need a heart full of grace. A soul generated by love." ~ Dr. Martin Luther King Jr.

Annie's Story

I know a family who moved from another State into a neighborhood near me several years ago. They had three young children, Annie was their middle child at age four. The family was in their new home for just a few months when Annie became ill.

A liver biopsy showed evidence that Annie was in end stage liver failure. She would die in less than 48 hours without a transplant. Friends and family of all faiths came together to help, serve and support her family.

Many people stepped up to be tested in case they could donate part of a liver to help Annie. Teenagers babysat the other children until late into the many nights that followed, while Annie's parents stayed with her at the hospital.

Friends and neighbors held garage sales, and people made candy and desserts to raise money for the family. A friend made a video explaining Annie's plight, which raised $10,000 alone.

Meals were prepared and steadily delivered to Annie's siblings at home, and to Annie's parents at the hospital. Women made blankets for Annie, and even a princess tiara for her hospital stay. Strangers prayed and fasted for a child they did not know.

The prayers and fasting worked. A liver from a deceased donor became available. It was a perfect match for Annie.

"It was through the sacrifice and love of so many people that we carried this burden," Annie's father said.

———

"In the end, the number of prayers we say may contribute to our happiness, but the number of prayers we answer may be of even greater importance." ~ Dieter F. Uchtdorf

The path to self-Love begins with service to others. The next step is to accept your circumstances, and accept who you are.

Acceptance ~

"Acceptance doesn't mean resignation. It means understanding that something is what it is, and there's got to be a way through it." ~ Michael J. Fox

Michael J. Fox has been an inspiration to me for many years.

As a young girl, I watched movies and television shows in which he starred, and fell in Love with his talent. He is a Canadian-American actor, author, comedian, producer, and now founder of the Michael J Fox Foundation to cure Parkinson's disease.

Michael J Fox starred in the movie "Back to the Future", and the television show, "Family Ties" where problems were solved or overcome in 30 to 90 minute scripted plots.

When he was diagnosed with Parkinson's disease in 1991, many realized that this problem would not be solved so readily.

By accepting his challenge, Michael J. Fox has shown that someone of small stature (he stands just 5'5") can be a very big man in his Love for life and family.

During the phase of my life when I was healing from abuse, my friend Carol made me a bookmark that read, "The only way out is through".

Carol also made me a Care Bear. Written in fabric paint on its tummy are the words, "One Step Closer".

Carol had been through challenges that most of us could not imagine. The manner in which she accepted and coped with her challenges is profoundly amazing.

She is a wonderful example of how to take one step closer to acceptance every day.

Saying Goodbye to Friends

Carol had 32 multiple personalities. Her mind fractured after a brutal rape and death by suffocation when she was three years old. Years later, she remembered that event under hypnosis. This is her recount, restated as I can recall.

"I was three years old, and at a house with lots of people. I was being punished for something and sent to a bedroom by myself. I was on the bed crying when I heard the door open. I looked up in time to see the torso of a man. He was wearing denim overalls. Instantly, something was put over my face – a pillow, I think."

Carol was suffocated to death by the pillow. She was never able to identify the man, having not seen his face. However, under hypnosis, Carol continues her account....

"I saw Heavenly Father. He was kind, and I was happy. He picked me up, and put me on his lap. He told me that something terrible had happened to me. He said that I had died.

"Heavenly Father also told me that I would need to go back. I didn't want to. I liked it here. He told me that I would not be alone when I went back. I would have friends to help me, and that they would be with me always.

"Just then, the angels began to sing. Heavenly Father said, 'They are singing carols. Just like your name is Carol'."

Carol remembers waking up in pain and lying on the bed in that room all alone. The carols she had heard had been replaced by voices. Voices in her head.

She was not afraid, and she never told anyone what had happened.

In fact, she quickly forgot the rape. The horrible memory was swallowed up by the 32 friends in her head, sent to protect her until she was strong enough to begin the healing process – until she was strong enough to ACCEPT her reality.

Thirty-two distinct, separate individuals accompanied Carol for her entire youth, and into her thirties. Carol was married, and had five children when I met her in group therapy. We, and many other women were healing from our abuse, but Carol was special. She was working on integrating each personality into her core self. This was difficult for Carol. Imagine killing off your 32 close friends.

Carol accepted the challenge. She had no idea what life would be like without Elizabeth, Mary, Tootie and Jake. Carol accepted that to truly heal, she would have to live life as Carol alone.

One of the most amazing experiences I've had in life was witnessing Carol's integration. I may be one of millions who has literally seen an individual ACCEPT her true self, and let go of aspects of life that were holding her back.

Under hypnosis, Carol saw each of her lifelong companions in her mind's eye. She approached them, thanked them, and hugged them. Then they each left Carol – in fact, integrated into Carol's self. For the first time ever, their traits became hers.

———

"There's no alternative to being yourself. Accept it, honor it, value it – and get on with it." ~ Rasheed Ogunlaru

"When you complain, you make yourself a victim. Leave the situation, change the situation, or accept it. All else is madness." ~ Eckhart Tolle

Accepting yourself, and your life, may not be as dramatic as it was for Carol. But it must be accomplished nonetheless. Let go of people, places, and situations that keep you from your own truth.

You may not have split personalities, but there are aspects of your life that do not encourage growth, improvement, and happiness. You know what they are, and you must get rid of them.

Face your problems, and hug them goodbye, realizing that they may have served a purpose, but the time has come when they are no longer needed.

Then, you must accept your imperfections, the fears you live with every day, and the ability you have to conquer them. The only way out is through.

Forgiveness ~

Forgiveness is not for the faint of heart. However it can be mastered with Sacrifice, Empowerment, and Love.

How does Sacrifice pertain to forgiveness? For me, it meant letting go of the pain and moving forward. No one else can move forward for me. I am not responsible for the offense perpetrated against me; but I am responsible for how I heal from it.

"To be wronged is nothing, unless you continue to remember it" ~ Confucius

There is no deadline for forgiveness.It's true though, that the sooner you forgive, the better off you'll be.

Childhood abuse requires therapy to heal. It may take many years before you are ready to forgive. And that's okay, as long as you know that is the goal.

If you work through the healing process with the idea that forgiveness is the whole reason for the healing – and in fact, the most important part of the healing – then you will come out stronger and better from your ordeal.

After years of imprisonment, Nelson Mandela said, "As I walked out of the door toward the gate that would lead to my freedom, I knew if I didn't leave my bitterness and hatred behind, I'd still be in prison".

Forgiveness can come very gradually. Many years after I completed my therapy, my husband asked me, "Do you feel like you've forgiven [your abuser]?"

I answered very quickly, "Yes, I have".

I hadn't realized that I had, but I found no animosity when I thought of him.

Then my husband asked, "Does he know that?"

Good question, dear. I had not considered why he would even need to know that I'd forgiven him, but he did. The next time I saw the man who had abused me for years, I offered him my forgiveness. He didn't say much. But his life changed.

Two years later he was living a life free of crime, drama, and heartache. He had overcome his own demons, and was living a life he could be proud of.

I learned that I had been holding him back by not forgiving. When you forgive, you change lives – yours and theirs.

"The practice of forgiveness is our most important contribution to the healing of the world."
~ Marianne Williamson

Empowerment and Love also come into play with forgiveness. Your forgiveness will not only Empower you, but it will Empower the one you forgive. I know this is true. Perhaps there is a little justice in this principle.

Perhaps as a victim, you lose a certain amount of power – especially in the case of abuse – but then you have the power to forgive. As the victim, you hold the power of forgiveness over your abuser.

My advice is to work toward feeling that forgiveness. Release that power, and Empower the lives of both you and those who have offended you. That is the purest form of Love that exists in our level of understanding.

"The weak can never forgive. Forgiveness is the attribute of the strong" ~ Mahatma Gandhi

While you're Empowering yourself by forgiving others, don't forget to forgive yourself. Many times we hold ourselves back because we cannot forgive our foolishness, our blunders, our mistakes, even our guilt. Forgiving ourselves is perhaps the most self-Empowering act we can take to better our own lives.

"I think that if God forgives us we must forgive ourselves. Otherwise, it is almost like setting up ourselves as a higher tribunal than Him" ~ C.S. Lewis

Forgive others and forgive yourself. The power you achieve will be unstoppable.

Engagement ~

In order to have a Love of self, you must be willing to engage in life. You must seek opportunities for growth and learning. By doing so, you will discover talents, skills, and passions you didn't know you had.

No matter what pain, fear, or misfortune you've experienced, don't let those aspects of life define who you are. You are more than the burdens you carry. Your misfortune allows you to have greater empathy and compassion for others. Learn to cut yourself some slack and engage!

"Life takes on meaning when you become motivated, set goals and charge after them in an unstoppable manner." ~ Les Brown

Test the power of YES! Opportunity often knocks through a question that sounds like, "Would you.....?"

By saying "Yes" you open your life to more knowledge, experience and value. You have more power simply saying "Yes".

"Striving for excellence motivates you; striving for perfection is demoralizing." ~ Harriet Braiker

Continue your odyssey of *exceptional leadership* and self-Love with full engagement, and yet realize that perfection is not possible.

It would be really boring anyway. How much fun would life be if you had nothing to improve?

"The most important thing in the Olympic Games is not to win but to take part, just as the most important thing in life is not the triumph but the struggle. The essential thing is not to have conquered but to have fought well." ~ Pierre de Coubertin

What does it mean to fight well? Og Mandino gives the answer:

If I feel depressed I will sing.
If I feel sad I will laugh.
If I feel ill I will double my labour.

If I feel fear I will plunge ahead.
If I feel inferior I will wear new garments.
If I feel uncertain I will raise my voice.
If I feel poverty I will think of wealth to come.
If I feel incompetent I will think of past success.
If I feel insignificant I will remember my goals.
Today I will be the master of my emotions.

Where will you be a year from today? If you don't engage life, then you will likely be in the same place you are right now. And a year from now, you will wish you had engaged TODAY.

Love yourself. Love your struggles. Love your happiness. Love who you are, and what you have been. Love the person you can, and will be. Love your talents, and the ones you gain when you follow the four steps of self-Love:

Service-**A**cceptance-**F**orgiveness-**E**ngagement

That is the way to SAFEly travel on your odyssey to SELF.

I've spent several paragraphs talking about self-Love. To some, that is the hardest kind of Love to have, and to feel. It is easier to feel Love for others. That being said, it's worth addressing to some degree.

How do we show charity and brotherly kindness to others? How can doing so achieve your goal of becoming an *exceptional leader*?

According to Gallup's widely respected *State of the American Workplace Report*, disengaged employees cost businesses $450-$550 billion a year in lost productivity.

Emotionally connected employees simply perform better. The Boston Consulting Group reports that since 2001, companies that embrace "whole person" employee engagement have consistently outpaced growth in S & P average cumulative share price by margins of up to 99 percent.

Gallup reports these additional benefits from total quality of life programs:

- 37% lower absenteeism
- 10% higher customer satisfaction
- Up to 22% higher profitability

"I am not sure exactly what heaven will be like, but I know that when we die and it comes time for God to judge us, he will not ask, 'How many good things have you done in your life?' rather he will ask, 'how much love did you put into what you did'?" ~ Mother Teresa

"It is good to love many things, for therein lies the true strength, and whosoever loves much performs much, and can accomplish much, and what is done in love is well done." ~ Vincent van Gogh

The *Unlimited Love Institute* researched the question: Does the unselfish Love of others contribute to the happiness, health and resilience of those who give it?

They discovered the answer is YES....

"We believe that contributing to the lives of others, so long as the giver maintains balance and boundaries so as not to become overwhelmed and exhausted, allows those who "love their neighbor" to flourish. They flourish by living an active life of giving not because they expect to be paid back in kind, but because in "doing unto others" they are freed from pre-occupation with the self and the problems of the self, from self-destructive emotions (like bitterness, rage, rumination, hos-tility, despair, and the like), from lack of purpose, and from loneliness or isolation.

Yes, certain individuals are called to special forms of love activism in which risk might find them, but risk is not sought after so much as accepted with courage.

Darwinians may love to study bees that sting and die for the hive, but this model has distorted our thinking about human altruism and flourishing.

We much prefer the founder of modern sociology, Comte, who simply contrasted the emptiness of an egoistic life with the fullness of an "other-regarding" one.

As the Jewish philosopher Martin Buber noted, there are two ways of living in the world. We can pretend that we are the center of the uni-

verse and relate to others only so long as they contribute to our egotistic agendas ("I-It"). If we live this way we will eventually fail.

Or we can realize that we are not the center of the universe and we can relate to others in love and respect ("I-Thou").

One wants to remember that Ebenezer Scrooge was miserable in his miserliness, but as he discovered how to freely give he also became so very joyful. Indeed, by the end of the story he has what I call "the giver's glow" and becomes one of the merriest of people.

So our Institute has a motto that Sir John Templeton approved for it: "In the giving of self lies the unsought discovery of a deeper self."

There you have it – scientific proof that LOVE matters! And it's important to SELF!

The *Unlimited Love Institute* researched a second question: Can the Spirituality of Unlimited Love Uplift the Workplace & Encourage Philanthropy?

Again, the answer is YES!

Institute Advisor Jo-Ann Triner noted, *"Work at the highest level is possible only when the inner person of heart and soul arrives in tandem with the outer person. Without it, we can be present yet bring only half ourselves to the task.*

We can be dutiful and diligent but not whole-hearted and human, working more like machines than men and women of soul and sub-stance. We can be exceptionally accomplished but not caring. We can act like professionals without the empathy and compassion of a true professional."

"Detached from this spiritual center, we may feel a deep sense of disillusionment and loss of meaning, immersed in the emptiness of it all.

To compensate for the lack, we may need many levels of management to do the heavy lifting that our hearts can do quite effortlessly and at no added expense. Cost-benefit studies bear this out."

The downside of ignoring spirituality and Love, she concludes, *"is the staggering cost of hiring, training and compensating a management hierarchy designed to accomplish nothing more than what a spiritually motivated work-force usually accomplishes on its own."*

Further research suggests: Spiritual practice in the workplace is associated with volunteering, employee health, and bottom-line success. In 2009, 41 percent of adult Americans volunteered for an average of 100 hours a year, or about two hours per week.

Fully 25 percent of all volunteering occurred through the workplace, where employees simply allowed people to take off for those couple of hours and help others in ways they found meaningful.

The result....

68%   said they felt physically healthier
96%   felt happier
73%   felt less stressed
100% felt relationships were more meaningful

Charitable Love makes a difference. Brotherly Love matters. Loving your neighbor has a tangible outcome. Nothing else matters if you don't have charity.

"The opposite of love is not hate, it's indifference. The opposite of art is not ugliness, it's indifference. The opposite of faith is not heresy, it's indifference. And the opposite of life is not death, it's indifference." ~ Elie Wiesel

"Love is not affectionate feeling, but a steady wish for the loved person's ultimate good as far as it can be obtained." ~ C.S. Lewis

Exceptional leadership requires LOVE. It requires Love of self, and charitable Love for others. As you continue your odyssey to SELF consider your need to improve your ability to Love.

An *exceptional leader* will possess not only self Love, but charitable, brotherly Love as well. You can be perfect in your ability to Love.

Charity never faileth. Go forward on your odyssey with that knowledge. Love is service. Love is acceptance. Love is forgiveness. Love is engagement.

You are going to LOVE the benefits you gain as you journey toward SELF Centered Leadership.

Chapter 5

*F*riendship

If I said, "5th grade, age 11," what memories would that conjure? Would they be good, or not so good?

For me, that period of life was more fear than fun; more sadness than laughter; more loneliness than Love. My parents were fighting incessantly, I was starting to mature physically, and my older siblings were making choices that added stress and anger to the household.

Age 11 was not a time I would want to repeat, and I have some regrets.

The Sting

I grew up on the Sonoran Desert. Scorpions, tarantulas and snakes were my playthings. Here's an interesting fact about scorpions - the smaller they are, the deadlier their venom. I respected their power, and left them alone.

Lexie was in my class at school. She was small, but tough. I was an averaged size 11 year-old, and Lexi was a foot shorter than me. Most school bullies were boys, but Lexi had venom to match those small scorpions. She became a bully when she was around her older sister, Martina.

Martina was two years older and three feet taller than Lexi. She was taller than everyone at school, even the boys. Martina was intimidating and mean. She coaxed Lexi to tease other kids.

Debbie was another school friend. She was...well, "homely". She was unassuming, modest, and plain. She wore dresses with pinafores and ankle socks. Not 1970's "cool".

She was polite – saying "please, sir" and "thank you, ma'am". If Lexie was a scorpion, Debbie was a puppy. Her naiveté left her vulnerable to victimization.

The day I allowed Debbie to be a victim, is a day I still regret.

Debbie and I rode the same bus that Lexi and Martina did, but we left the bus two stops before them. On this day, either Lexi and Martina planned to get off at our stop, or the following events prompted a change in plans. Whatever the cause, there was definitely an effect.

Debbie sat with me near the front of the bus. Lexi, Martina, and their Friends talked loudly and profanely at the back. A typical ride home from school.

As the bus approached our stop, Lexi came down the

aisle and tripped on Debbie's foot. Lexi fell face down into the aisle as the bus stopped. Martina screamed obscenities and raced to Lexi.

Debbie graciously apologized and picked up Lexie's books from the aisle. Lexi wasn't really hurt, and Martina was taking care of her, so Debbie and I walked off the bus.

Before the bus doors were closed, Martina, Lexi, and a few tough girls Martina's age, left the bus behind us.

"You tripped my sister!" Martina yelled. The bus driver pulled away.

"I didn't mean to," Debbie said. "It was an accident".

"My sister should beat you up for that."

Debbie repeated, "I'm sorry. I didn't do it on purpose."

"Beat her up, Lexi!" shouted Martina, pushing Lexi and Debbie together.

Lexi threw a punch at Debbie's face. It met its mark. Debbie whined in pain. Lexi is egged on by Martina and her Friends.

Debbie tried holding up her books to shield the blows, but Lexi was more determined. Her books were knocked to the ground.

She rolled into a ball. Lexi began kicking her, covering Debbie's pink gingham dress, socks and shoes in dirt.

Some kids from our stop spread out into a large circle. Others left the scene altogether. I just stood there.

A police car came into view down the street. Lexi, her sister and Friends hopped a fence to a vacant field.

The officer helped a crying Debbie into his car. She got a ride home. It was over, and I had done nothing to help my Friend.

I don't know why I hadn't done anything. Was I afraid to become a target myself? Lexi had never picked a fight with me before that day, but she may have while under her sister's influence.

I had great empathy for Debbie. I knew what it was like to be a victim. I prayed every night that *I* would be saved from *my* abuse.

What if I was supposed to be an answer to Debbie's prayer? I had acted badly.

—

The fact remains, I hadn't done anything to stop an injustice. I regret my inaction to this very day. I hate that I was not courageous, and that I did not stand up in support of my Friend.

Debbie was not seriously hurt, but she lost a chunk of her innocence that day. She didn't deserve such treatment by Lexi, but she did deserve to have a better Friend in me.

"The only way to have a friend is to be one." ~ Ralph Waldo Emerson

Charles Darwin said, *"A man's friendships are the best measure of his worth"*. While I don't agree with all of Charles Darwin's scientific findings, his words about Friendship are relevant. True Friendship is a relationship that evolves over time.

What does Friendship really mean?

How do you become a Friend? How do you increase your worth by having meaningful Friendships?

The purpose of this book is to help you become a greater leader of SELF, but no one gets through life, or leads completely by themselves. Even the greatest leaders in history have expressed gratitude for Friends and partners who influenced their odyssey to SELF.

You cannot be successful in ANYTHING without assistance from SOMEONE.

"Of all the things which wisdom provides to make us entirely happy, much the greatest is the possession of friendship." ~ Epicurus

Wisdom is a great asset in leadership, but exceptional leadership cannot exist without Friendship.

"The Top 10 Greatest Leaders of All Time" list was recently published on OMGTopLists.com. George Washington, the first President of the United States and one of its founding fathers, is ranked first on the list.

Did George Washington have Friends? YES!

George William Fairfax, a Friend from Washington's youth in Virginia, who became Washington's mentor.

Henry Lee, a Friend from the neighborhood of Washington's home in Mount Vernon, who later served under Washington during the Revolution.

General Henry Knox also served under George Washington during the Revolution, and later became the Secretary of War. Their Friendship lasted for 25 years.

George Washington said of General Knox:

"There is no man in the United States with whom I have been in habits of greater intimacy, no one whom I have loved more sincerely, nor any for whom I have had a greater friendship".

I give credit to George Washington for developing Friendships during a time of extreme stress such as war. Perhaps Friendships during these times are the most enduring and trustworthy.

Nelson Mandela is the number 5 leader on OMGTopList.com's *"Greatest Leaders of All Time."* He was a South African anti-apartheid revolutionary who later served as President of that country.

Did Nelson Mandela have Friends? YES!

An article titled "Still Fighting For His Friend", in the July 2013 issue of *The Economist*, noted that:

In 1964, as Nelson Mandela prepared to make the most important speech of his life, three words were introduced at the last minute by his lawyer and friend, George Bizos.

Mandela was facing the death penalty in a case brought by the apartheid regime in Africa. The additional words were "if needs be" and signaled to the judges that Mandela was not seeking martyrdom. To widespread surprise and relief, Mr. Mandela and the other nine accused were spared execution and sentenced to life imprisonment instead.

Mandela's friend may have indeed saved his life.

"Be true to your work, your word, and your friend." ~ John Boyle O'Reilly

A deep and meaningful Friendship formed between U.S. President Franklin D. Roosevelt and British Prime Minister Winston Churchill in December 1941 at the First Washington Conference. The bond between the two world leaders was almost instant, and they even delivered a Christmas greeting to the United States and the world from the White House December 24th of that year.

The two statesman made many joint appearances and worked together to plan strategy and victory for their allies during World War II. FDR and Churchill came to rely on each other as Friends.

Churchill wrote about FDR, "I felt I was in contact with a very great man who was also a warm-hearted friend and the foremost champion of the high causes which we served".

Leaders must have Friends, and leaders must be Friends. There are, however, many who believe that Friendship is in crisis today.

Could that be the reason that exceptional leadership is also waning?

A 2013 nation-wide study by *Life Boat – Friends at Their Best* revealed a Friendship crisis in America. The homepage of their website states: "*Only a quarter of adults report being truly satisfied with their friendships. And almost two-thirds lack confidence in even their closest friends. Facing this, most Americans — by more than 2 to 1 — say they'd prefer to have deeper friendships than more friends.*"

The study tells us what people look for in Friends:

- Loyalty – 81%
- A decent, good person – 80%
- Will be there is crisis – 74%
- Likes me – 73%
- Is fun to be with - 68%

We also learn what people DON'T look for in Friends:

- See this person often – 31%
- Shares spiritual/religious beliefs – 25%
- Help getting ahead in career – 21%
- Same political view – 17%
- Physically attractive – 14%

In other words, the Friendships that influence us the most are with people who will Sacrifice for us, Empower us, and Love us. You may not have realized it, but you've been looking for Friends who are exceptional leaders. You want Friends you can trust, and with whom you can make enjoyable memories.

On the converse side, we don't choose our Friends because they live next door; or because they believe exactly as we do; or because we can use their influence to our gain. The best Friendships are not formed for selfish reasons, but they are indeed SELF-ish!

How do you know you have true Friends? Is there someone you could call during the middle of the night if you needed help? That person is likely a true Friend.

Is there someone whom you could share your deepest dreams with? Is there someone you feel you can be completely honest with? Are there people who Love you as your genuine self? These are your true Friends.

What can you do to deepen your Friendships with these individuals? How can you be a better Friend yourself?

Peter Pal

In the early 1990's, my family and I lived in Kirkland, Washington. We would occasionally answer a knock on the door to find Peter Pal.

Peter Pal was a hand-made stuffed doll that someone made for a specific, single purpose. Their objective was to anonymously provide fun and feelings of Love for their Friends. Peter Pal was always holding a plate of goodies – cookies, brownies, etc.

There was always a note pinned to Peter with instructions to pass him along to someone else with a special plate of goodies from you.

It was fun to try and guess who left Peter Pal and his goodies on our porch. However, the greatest fun came in deciding which fabulous treat we would make and deliver to someone we loved.

—

I have no idea who started Peter Pal, but I know my family was Loved. Peter Pal visited our home on at least three different occasions. Is there a Friend, or a group of Friends you can start this fun tradition with?

My family has been in need many times, such as when my husband was unemployed, we were bankrupt, or were merely experiencing a bump in the road. In almost every situation, when Friends found out about our plight, food, gifts, or money were secretly delivered to us.

One Christmas, when we were down and just about out, someone anonymously delivered all the ingredients for a Christmas dinner, plus toys for the kids, gift cards for us, and $500 cash.

We still don't know who gave us such an unexpected miracle, but we are so grateful for the Love that was shown. We were able to have hope for a little longer because a Friend took action.

"Friendship is unnecessary, like philosophy, like art...it has no survival value; rather it is one of those things that give value to survival." ~ C. S. Lewis

When a Friend of yours is merely "surviving", I encourage you to take action that will bring them hope.

Geez buddy, what's your problem?

One evening many years ago, my husband, two kids, and I, left home in our car. Just a block past our home, we noticed a large, dark vehicle driving closely behind us.

Their headlights shone into the rearview mirror of the car I was driving, causing the bright reflection to blind me a little.

As I sped up to get out of the blinding light of the other

car, I noticed that the driver behind me sped up as well. I didn't recognize the car, so my first reaction was anger at this impatient person who obviously was in a hurry to get somewhere. The driver could not pass me on the one-lane highway.

The driver pursued us very closely for the next two miles, occasionally blinking the car's lights. We were concerned about the possibility of road rage.

As we approached a traffic light, I veered into the left lane, and noticed the car behind us was going to pass us on the right. Just about then, the light turned red, and both cars had to stop.

I looked over at the other driver, ready to give a look as if to say, "Geez, buddy, what's your problem?"

Just then, the driver rolled down her window. It was our neighbor and Friend, Linda. Laughing, she said, "We're trying to bring you brownies!"

———

What great Friends! They were willing to follow us for miles just to bring us a treat.

I've learned that we often discount the service our Friends provide us; or we get so busy with our own agenda, that we miss out completely.

When I want to take action to help Friends, I'm not always sure what I can do. It's common to say, "Let me know if I can help." Although people appreciate that sentiment, they may not even know how others can help.

During six weeks of recovery from surgery years ago, a good Friend of mine came over and made my bed for me. Seriously. She made my bed. It was the sweetest gesture imaginable at the time. I couldn't make my bed myself, yet she knew how important it was to me.

That Friend probably doesn't realize how meaningful that simple act of kindness was to me. Many times we think that service has to be something big. Typically, the smallest acts are the most appreciated.

The Friend Blog on Lifeboat Friends at Their Best website, published an article titled, *Stop Asking, "How Can I Help?"* The list provides ways to serve your friends when they're in need, because sometimes we want to help, but don't know how. (See #2 on *The Rest of the Story* page at the end of this book)

"But it all comes down to friendship, treating people right." ~ Ernie Banks

Let's review the results of the *Life Boat – Friends at Their Best* study - what people want in Friends...

- Loyalty – 81%
- A decent, good person – 80%
- Will be there in crisis – 74%
- Likes me – 73%
- Is fun to be with - 68%

Apply this knowledge on your quest toward exceptional leadership. As you are more loyal, more decent and good, available in crisis, likeable, and fun, you will find your influence on others will feel more like a Friendship than a relationship of leadership.

If you knew a leader genuinely cared for you, wouldn't you be more likely to follow through with assignments and tasks at his or her request?

Gallup's 2013 *State of the American Workplace Report* states only 30 percent of the workforce is engaged. The report suggests 20 percent of American workers have bosses from hell who make them miserable. And 50 percent of workers are just kind of present at work, but not inspired by their work or managers.

Gallup found that managers who focus on their employees' strengths can practically eliminate active disengagement and double the average of U.S. workers who are engaged nationwide.

Exceptional leadership is using natural *influence* combined with actionable *intention* to inspire one or more people to affect change in the life of someone else.

Exceptional leadership is not just about teaching someone to lead. It's about teaching someone how to inspire someone else to lead. *Exceptional leadership* is the *intention* to develop more leaders, not just *influence* followers.

Imagine what the U.S. workforce would look like if people in positions of leadership were actively working toward achieving *exceptional leadership*!

Managers and leaders should focus on ways to connect with each employee. Applying principles of Friendship is a way to shape a team member's workplace experience. A leader's interaction with an employee has the potential to influence his or her engagement.

"A true friend freely advises justly, assists readily, adventures boldly, takes all patiently, defends courageously, and continues a friend unchangeably." ~ William Penn

Make sure you are building Friendships. The Friends you make may be the people who help you progress in your career, volunteer work, and your family life.

Job seekers today search the internet for employment opportunities. Conversations with a potential employer may no longer happen until the interview. IF you get to interview.

Word of mouth is key to finding a job today. People we know, know someone who can help us. Friends help Friends find jobs, marriage partners and opportunities.

Where would we be without Friends?

When I began therapy to overcome childhood abuse, I learned the ultimate goal - to confront my abuser face to face. I never imagined I could. On the day I met that goal, a friend was at my side.

I read the letter I'd written to the man who traumatized my childhood. She didn't say anything. She was just present. That's all I needed.

When have you needed a Friend to just be present?

On your odyssey, be a Friend, make Friends and value Friendships. Employees, employers, team members, family members, neighbors and associates are your Friends.

Exceptional leaders recognize the responsibility they have to influence Friends.

Exceptional leaders influence their Friends to achieve worthwhile results.

Exceptional leaders help their Friends develop into exceptional leaders.

Jackie Bailey

Chapter 6

My SELF Fulfillment

The odyssey in my fishbowl has been fraught with danger. It has also included joys and triumphs.

The sails on my boat have been Sacrifice, Empowerment, Love and Friendship. I've felt like jumping ship many times. I don't swim well, so I've thought better of it.

I've not always stayed on course, but I've never drifted beyond the ability to come back. I don't believe that's possible. We can always come back.

People and opposing forces have tried to pull me down. I have resisted. I have endured. I have stayed afloat.

Before I conclude this chapter and this book, I share two experiences that testify of truths I've learned while on my odyssey. I KNOW the following:

I KNOW there is a God, and He KNOWS me!

I KNOW that bumps can be blessings!

I Could Gopher Some Revenge

I was just married, and working to complete 160 required hours of externship to graduate dental assistant school. I was at the dental office of Dr. Small. This was not really his name, but it describes him perfectly.

He was a man of little integrity. He made rude comments to his staff, and rude comments about his wife to staff members.

On this morning while assisting Dr. Small with a dental patient, I told the following story:

"We were driving through Dome Valley. We noticed a snake curled up in the road. Arny stopped next to the snake. He opened his door to see it up close. It was a large gopher snake warming itself in the sun.

It began to slither toward, and under, our car. When it didn't slither out the other side, Arny left the car to investigate. He could not see the snake anywhere.

Getting on his hands and knees, Arny realized the snake had disappeared into the engine of our car! How far, he couldn't tell.

"We closed the vents. Could the snake get into the car? We didn't know. Arny started driving slowly, hoping to kill it, or coax it out of its hiding place".

"As we drove, we could hear a thump, thump underneath the car. Another driver approached us from behind. He could see what was happening, and pulled up next to our car".

"There's a snake wrapped around your axle," he said. "I think he's trying to get out."

"We kept driving slowly. The thumping became louder and louder....then silent. The other driver followed us, watching. He told us the snake had broken up into pieces and was scattered along the road."

When I finished telling my story to Dr. Small, he said, "That is the biggest load of crap I've ever heard. No snake is going to crawl up inside a car like that. You are such a liar!"

It wasn't enough to insult me in front of just one patient, but Dr. Small mentioned my "dishonesty" to other patients and staff members throughout the day. He enjoyed belittling me.

At the end of the day, it was typical for Dr. Small to leave when the last patient was gone. The staff would stay to clean, and prepare for the next day. Today, Dr. Small left the office when we left.

We walked together out the back door where our cars were parked. Right away we saw it, coiled up in the alley between us and our vehicles.

Dr. Small's office was located in the city. Wildlife sightings were rare. Today, there was a gopher snake in that alley. What were the odds of THAT?

Dr. Small retrieved a broom inside the office and tried to sweep the snake out of our way. It slithered toward our cars instead. It made a beeline for Dr. Small's Porsche Carrera. It went under his car, and he waited for it to appear on the other side. It didn't.

He went down on his hands and knees, looking under his car. The snake had disappeared into the underside of his Porsche. He jumped in and closed the vents.

While Dr. Small uttered profanities at the snake that he couldn't find, I got in my car and drove home.

—

God was aware of my situation that day. He understood that I was being belittled and called out unfairly. He intervened on my behalf. There is no other explanation.

I felt, and witnessed His influence. I KNOW God lives, and that He KNOWS me. He also knows YOU.

When You Knee'd A Little Relief

That day at camp, all 75 girls in our charge were playing games in an open field. I was watching the activity of the 14-year olds. I saw Katie running, then fall.

When I approached, I could see her knee was dislocated. Katie was pale and grimacing in pain. The nearest medical clinic was 5 miles outside of camp. We needed to get her there before she went into shock.

Katie was helped into an SUV, and laid across one seat. I sat near her. The dirt road to our destination was full of ruts. Every jarring move of the car would cause pain in her knee.

The driver attempted to avoid hitting the potholes in the road. She drove slowly, trying to keep Katie comfortable.

After a 20 minute session exercising the shock absorbers, and believing the roughest patch of road was behind us, the driver accelerated.

I saw the large pothole ahead. The driver didn't. We hit it going about thirty miles an hour. We were airborne. I looked down at Katie to warn her, but she already knew, and she was ready.

She screamed in pain as we touched down.

Then Katy said, "Oh…that feels better."

Amazingly, that bump relocated Katie's knee. Her pain was relieved.

———

We go through life so eager to have smooth sailing, and avoid bumps in our path, that we may not recognize that bumps can be blessings. Avoiding bumps may keep us from having what we hope for.

Sacrifice of your time, energy and talents may seem like bumps to avoid. However, if I had not spent time, energy and talent to help others during the hardest times of my odyssey, I would not have had faith necessary unto life.

Healing from abuse, and Forgiving hurtful offenses may seem like bumps to avoid. However, without accepting my circumstances, realizing that I could conquer them, and enduring the pain of therapy, I would not have experienced the joy of seeing change in my life, and the life of another.

Looking honestly at your weaknesses, flaws, and mistakes may be painful bumps to avoid. However, if Carol hadn't accepted her past with all its pain and sorrow, and then fought the tough fight to change it, she would not be the whole person she is today.

Two things I know – that God is aware of us and will support us in our good choices; and very often the bumps He places in our path are blessings in disguise.

Discover your truths – truths learned by experience and hardships. This knowledge is the rudder of your vessel that will guide your current and future odyssey.

Keep this in mind as you travel. Your Odyssey is not easy. It's not supposed to be. We learn from challenges we experience. Lessons we learn will influence the lives of others.

Hoist your sails with excitement and anticipation. Practice SELF awareness, SELF-ishness, and SELF centeredness. Master Sacrifice, Empowerment, Love and Friendship.

"A leader is one who knows the way, goes the way, and shows the way" ~ John C. Maxwell

You KNOW the way. Others will act on your influence. Don't just lead them, SHOW them how to be an exceptional leader – just as you've become!

SELFCentered Leadership

Becoming Influential, Intentional & Exceptional

Jackie Bailey

Jackie Bailey

The Rest of the Story

1. Obituary for Elizabeth Sleasman on ObitsforLife.com. Message from Elizabeth:

I ask that EVERY parent and grandparent show this to their teens, even if they are perfect children. I was a perfect daughter, and my parents never knew I was using and drinking for at least the first five years (age 12 to 17), then only suspected it until the last ten years of my life when I couldn't hide it any more.

Message to the teens: If you haven't started - don't. If you have, quit NOW. Your drinking/drug using friends are not really friends, they will steal from you, use you, and will do anything to get another "fix" - just like me.

What starts out as fun for the first year or so, ends up to be a horrible, lonely life. During the last ten years, I never knew from one day to the next where I was going to be, I ate out of garbage cans, begged, and stole. I slept in bushes, doorways, abandoned vehicles, and nearly froze to death in the winter.

Most of the time I was high or coming down, and much of that time, did not know what I was saying or doing - I could remember very little of what happened the night before. While using, I thought I was invincible and nothing could ever happen to me - after all, I was the "safest" user out there.

I had a little girl who, because of my drinking and

drugging was born with fetal alcohol syndrome and other very serious problems. I did not believe this, I believed she was perfect and only a little slow; and of course, it was not my fault - she will need specialized care for the rest of her life - again, not my fault, or so I thought.

You will become a thief and a liar, next you will lose your family, your "real" friends, and eventually your life. I started with Marijuana, and alcohol. It did not take very long for me to be so hooked on hard drugs that I could not have quit if I wanted to. Some of my closest "friends" overdosed and died; I did not quit. The light of my life, my daughter, was taken away - even then, I could not quit.

I entered the Methadone treatment and stopped using, but unfortunately my drinking habit kept on and I started using again.

More recently I was admitted to the hospital because I was vomiting blood - my stomach was raw and the lining split because of crystal meth and alcohol. The doctors glued it together, and tried to get me to go to treatment - I said I would do it myself.

I have quit now, but I am dead; don't wait as long as I did, give your life another chance.

2. *Stop Asking, "How Can I Help?"* from The Friend Blog on Lifeboat Friends at Their Best website:

A Friend gets sick:

"I just spent six months recovering from a bone marrow transplant. Whenever friends asked "How can I help?" I found it difficult to come up with an answer. It wasn't that there was a lack of things I needed. After all, this was a difficult time for me. But nothing felt like the right answer to give. So instead, I would just tell people I was doing fine.

However, the friends that showed up without asking transformed my recovery experience. There was the once-a-week voicemail to say I miss you. There was the perfect care package with my favorite food and trashy magazines. There were the hand painted pictures from my friends kids. And perhaps the most helpful of all were the unprompted offers to come for a visit, complete with suggested dates. When someone is going through something as tough as a medical recovery, take the work out if for them, and just jump in – it's the best medicine."
~ WOMAN, 32

A Friend has a new baby:

"Once you have kids, it's easy to sort of lose touch with your "previous" identity and feel like you're in full-time parent mode. What's great is when friends don't write you off socially — when they still invite you out to things or even make the effort to come hang out at your place. Of course you can't always make it, but it means a lot to still be invited. And sometimes it motivates us to rally... to get a babysitter, go out, and be our own people in the world again!" ~ MAN, 37

"Wanna know how to help a friend that is a new parent? One word. Food. Frozen food, groceries, takeout delivered from a favorite restaurant... Any form, just food, food and food. And don't feel weird about taking it over there. Contact your new parent friends and give them a couple of options when you can bring it by. (If they have pets, some treats for them would be very appreciated too)." ~ WOMAN, 37

A Friend loses a loved-one:

"When my sister passed away, I was comforted with support immediately. However six months later, the phone calls, supportive emails and cards had stopped. It made me really sad. I could have used a six-month "memory" day to talk about my sister, look at photos and share stories with my friends and family." ~ WOMAN, 69

A Friend is having problems with a child:

"People want to help you problem solve, but there is often a thinly-veiled judgment that if your kid has messed up, it's because you did something wrong and you're an inadequate parent. So don't judge; that alone is hugely helpful. The people who have helped the most have a direct connection with our kid, and they have engaged with him directly. That's been rare, but really valuable." ~ MAN, 58

A Friend is having relationship troubles:

"When I thought I was looking at a traumatic, sudden end to my marriage, I found I couldn't stand to be alone. But I also couldn't stand to feel so pathetic as to tell anyone that.

My best friends just showed up, some for an hour, some for a day, some for a weekend, and one for a few weeks, without making me ask. They showed up and didn't ask for anything of me other than my company, and they didn't freak out when I was crazy drunk or crazy sad or crazy mad. They were just there, and knew me well enough to know that's what I needed." ~ WOMAN, 39

A Friend is unemployed:

"You lose so many inputs when you're suddenly not involved in work anymore. All those people needing you for whatever — they are suddenly gone. It's like a vacuum. Friends who helped fill that up were a huge relief. One booked meetings with me a couple times in the first few weeks for advice and I loved that." ~ MAN, 35

Jackie Bailey

Sources

Allen West http://allenbwest.com/

American Academy of Environmental Medicine (AAEM) http://www.aaemonline.org/

Arthur Ashe Learning Center http://www.arthurashe.org

C.S.Lewis Biography http://www.biography.com/people/cs-lewis-9380969

Charles Darwin Biography http://www.biography.com/people/charles-darwin-9266433

Child Trends http://www.childtrends.org/

Childbearing Outside of Marriage. Estimates and Trends in the United States. http://www.childtrends.org/wp-content/uploads/2013/02/Child_Trends-2011_11_01_RB_NonmaritalCB.pdf

CLASP Center for Law and Social Policy Are Married Parents Really Better For Children? By Mary Parke http://www.clasp.org/admin/site/publications_states/files/0086.pdf

Confucius Biography http://www.biography.com/people/confucius-9254926

Dieter F. Uchtdorf https://www.lds.org/prophets-and-apostles/what-are-prophets/bio/dieter-f-uchtdorf

Disney Movies Official Site – Finding Nemo http://movies.disney.com/finding-nemo

Dwight D. Eisenhower
http://millercenter.org/president/eisenhower

Eckhart Tolle
http://www.eckharttolle.com/about/eckhart/

Elie Wiesel Biography
http://www.biography.com/people/elie-wiesel-9530714

Epicurus and Epicurean Philosophy
http://www.epicurus.net/

Ernie Banks http://baseballhall.org/hof/Banks-Ernie

Forbes Magazine, The World's Most Powerful
http://www.forbes.com/powerful-people/

Franklin D. Roosevelt Biography
http://www.biography.com/people/franklin-d-roosevelt-9463381

George Washington IStock Photo
http://www.istockphoto.com/photo/george-washington-17358200

GOOD- A magazine for the global citizen March 17, 2011
Heroes: Hear the Voice of the Heroic Young Woman Who
Saved Thousands of Lives
http://magazine.good.is/articles/heroes-hear-the-voice-of-the-young-heroic-woman-who-saved-thousands-of-lives

Harriet Braiker http://www.harrietbraiker.com/

Institute of Responsible Technology
http://www.responsibletechnology.org/

John Boyle O'Reilly

http://en.wikipedia.org/wiki/John_Boyle_O'Reilly

John C. Maxwell http://www.johnmaxwell.com/

John D. Rockefeller http://www.history.com/topics/john-d-rockefeller

John Henry Newman
http://www.cardinaljohnhenrynewman.com/

John Lennon http://www.johnlennon.com/biography

John Quincy Adams
http://millercenter.org/president/jqadams

Larry Bird
http://www.nba.com/history/players/bird_bio.html

Lectures On Faith Joseph Smith Harold B. Lee Library
http://eom.byu.edu/index.php/Lectures_on_Faith

Les Brown http://lesbrown.com/

Life Boat – Friends at Their Best Report: State of
Friendship http://getlifeboat.com/goodies/report2013/

Mahatma Gandhi
http://www.biography.com/people/mahatma-gandhi-9305898#!

Marianne Williamson http://www.marianne.com/

Martin Luther King, Jr. Biography
http://www.biography.com/people/martin-luther-king-jr-9365086

Martin Luther King, Jr
http://www.thekingcenter.org/about-dr-king

Michael J. Fox Biography
http://www.biography.com/people/michael-j-fox-9542279

Mother Teresa
http://www.biography.com/people/mother-teresa-9504160

National Vital Statistics Centers for Disease Control
December 2013
http://www.cdc.gov/nchs/data/nvsr/nvsr62/nvsr62_09.pdf

Nelson Mandela
http://www.nelsonmandela.org/content/page/biography

Nelson Mandela IStock Photo
http://www.istockphoto.com/photo/nelson-mandela-18888330

Norman Schwarzkopf
http://www.biography.com/people/norman-schwarzkopf-9476401

Obits for Life Elizabeth Sleasman
http://www.obitsforlife.com/obituary/749511/Sleasman-Elizabeth.php

Og Mandino http://intentionalcreation.com/about-og-mandino/

OMGTopLists.com 10-16-14
http://www.omgtoplists.com/history/top-10-greatest-leaders-of-all-time/

Oprah Winfrey Biography
http://www.biography.com/people/oprah-winfrey-9534419

Pierre de Coubertin
http://www.coubertin.ch/e/cipc003.htm

ProCon.org http://www.procon.org/

Prominent Russians- Nikolai Vavilov
http://russiapedia.rt.com/prominent-russians/science-and-technology/nikolay-vavilov/

Ralph Waldo Emerson Biography
http://www.biography.com/people/ralph-waldo-emerson-9287153

Rasheed Ogunlaru http://www.rasaru.com/

Rick Rescorla Memorial http://rickrescorla.com/

Seed The Untold Story http://www.seedthemovie.com/

Single Parent Households – How Does it Affect the Children? http://www.st-andrew-online.org/docs/marriageconv5.pdf

State of the American Workforce Report Gallup
http://www.gallup.com/strategicconsulting/163007/state-american-workplace.aspx

The Economist July 21st, 2013 Still Fighting For His Friend
http://www.economist.com/blogs/baobab/2013/07/interview-george-bizos

The Unlimited Love Institute
http://unlimitedloveinstitute.org/love-happiness/

The Virgin Diet. JJ Virgin http://thevirgindiet.com/

Thomas Edison Biography
http://www.biography.com/people/thomas-edison-

9284349

Tony Dungy http://www.coachdungy.com/

Vincent van Gogh Biography
http://www.biography.com/people/vincent-van-gogh-9515695

Walt Disney Biography
http://www.biography.com/people/walt-disney-9275533

William Penn Biography
http://www.biography.com/people/william-penn-9436869#synopsis

Winston Churchill Biography
http://www.biography.com/people/winston-churchill-9248164

Zig Ziglar http://www.ziglar.com/

About the Author

Jackie Bailey is the President of Emerald City Consulting, and the writer of *Navigating Your Fishbowl*, a leadership blog. She is a professional speaker, business consultant, and leadership coach.

For more than 30 years, Jackie has led teams of various sizes. Some teams with as few as three people, while others as large as 100.

Because of her outstanding team leadership, Jackie was awarded the 2011 Excellence in Marketing Award; and 2012 Excellence in Education and Training Award from Toastmasters International.

Today, Jackie works with business owners, teams, and individuals to increase leadership, communication and engagement. She helps organizations enhance communication, optimize individual performance, and increase team effectiveness.

Contact Jackie Bailey when you need a dynamic speaker at your event or conference; when recruiting a new team member; and when your current team needs to be more influential, intentional and exceptional.

www.EmeraldCityConsulting.com
jackie@EmeraldCityConsulting.com
www.NavigatingYourFishbowl.com

425-894-3424

Jackie Bailey

Made in the USA
Middletown, DE
29 June 2015